in our shoes

real life issues
for Ministers' Wives
by Ministers' Wives

Rachel Lovingood • Jennifer Landrith

LifeWay Press®
Nashville, Tennessee

D1410102

Published by LifeWay Press®
© 2008 Jennifer Landrith and Rachel Lovingood
Reprinted 2016

ISBN 9781415866498
Item 005183353

Dewey decimal: 253.2
Subject heading: MINISTERS' WIVES \ WOMEN \ WIVES

To order additional copies of this resource: write LifeWay Church Resources Customer Service; One LifeWay Plaza; Nashville, Tn 37234-0113; fax order to 615.251.5933; call toll free 800.458.2772; email orderentry@lifeway.com; order online www.lifeway.com; or visit the LifeWay Christian Store serving you.

Printed in the United States of America

Leadership and Adult Publishing
LifeWay Church Resources
One LifeWay Plaza
Nashville, TN 37234-0152

contents

The Authors

Jennifer Landrith (right) served alongside her husband David for 27 years before he passed away. The last 17 years of their ministry was spent at Long Hollow Baptist, Hendersonville, Tennessee where David was pastor. They have three children, Rachel, Sam, and Josh. Jennifer has been a conference leader helping ministers' wives and has a passion for encouraging other wives in ministry as they serve.

Rachel Lovingood (left) is the Senior Associate Pastor's wife and a women's leader at First Baptist Church, Cleveland, Tennessee, the mom of three fantastic kids, and a LifeWay Ministry Multiplier. She is the lead writer for Impact Resources and has also written *Even MORE* and *Salvaging My Identity* for teenage girls and young women. She uses her passion for Christ, her energetic style, and her sometimes crazy sense of humor to encourage and teach women to find the answers they need from the only true source of wisdom—the Bible.

Introduction

Have you ever heard the old saying, "Don't judge me until you've walked a mile in my shoes"? This quip explains, perhaps more accurately than anything else, the unique challenges faced by those married to ministers. Though life in ministry ideally should be a positive and exciting experience, it often gets a bad rap. Serving alongside a husband committed to church service is no small task. It takes courage, adaptability, and a heart centered on pleasing God and loving people—even when some of those people aren't so lovable.

As ministry wives we've found few resources to help us deal with the specific and unusual situations we encounter. That's why we desire to provide a Bible study that encourages and equips fellow ministry wives as they draw closer in their relationships with the Lord. We've designed this study to help you see the blessings and influence that are uniquely yours because of the call that God has placed on you. We hope that as you find opportunity to connect with other ministry wives, you will find encouragement for your own journey.

As you read, know that we do walk in shoes similar to yours. We are friends who've been ministers' wives for over 40 combined years. We grew up in the same youth group, married best friends, and currently serve alongside each other at Long Hollow Baptist Church in

Hendersonville, Tennessee. Although our lives share many similarities, our journeys to this point differ.

I (Rachel) am married to Jeff, and we have enjoyed the privilege of ministering to teenagers for over 20 years. He has served as student minister at many different churches of various sizes and demographics. Through the years and the moves across country, I've dealt with lots of transitions and worked with different staff situations. While raising three children and freelance writing for various publications, I still try to stay connected and very involved with our church's youth as well as its Women's Ministry.

I (Jennifer) am married to David and we, too, have served for over 20 years while rearing three children. I know what it's like to be the only staff wife as well as being a part of a large group of staff wives. Through the years I've felt the pressures of supporting a husband who's pastored churches of 100 as well as a church of over 4,000. I have served in ministries of the church from preschool to students and enjoy involvement in those as well as Women's Ministry.

As your friends on this journey, we hope to address many of the situations facing you and your life in ministry. Know that while our study is not all-inclusive, the topics we will address in each chapter are chosen with you in mind.

How to Use This Study

This book is divided into eight chapters that can be completed for personal enrichment or as a guide to build discussions and interactions with a group of ministers' wives (see Leader Guide). You'll also find a section called Hot Topics which addresses real-life questions from ministers' wives across the country. Helpful Hints are also provided at the back of the book. This section is full of valuable information on everything from buying deacon gifts to helpful cooking hints that will help you prepare for unexpected company. You may wish to do one section a day, one a week, or even one a month. The material is flexible; make it work for you.

Remember, too, that we can often learn from talking with others who share situations similar to our own. Consider connecting with other ministry wives in one of the following ways:

- Host a monthly party for the staff wives at your church. Use this material to build and strengthen the team. Choose to sit down and really get to know one another. You'll learn to continually encourage one another on a deeper level.

- Plan a denominational or associational dinner. Find other wives at sister churches in your area who could benefit from this project. Select highlights from the content and find fun ways to share it with them during a relaxing evening of food and fellowship.

- Form an online community. Use the study as a springboard for thought to connect with others—regardless of location—in a safe and confidential environment. Share what you learn from this study. Ask for tips and offer support.

- Create a book club for ministers' wives. Get together with other ministry wives and chat at a coffee shop or take turns meeting at each others' homes. Use this book as your first discussion piece as you talk about a different chapter each meeting. Then, if the group wants to continue, find other books on relevant topics.

- Hold a community-wide, interdenominational picnic or tea. Use this event as a tool to bridge the denominational boundaries in your community and collect information on ladies interested in doing the study. Find a time to meet and plan a format that works for the group.

- Use for gifts and outreach. Take copies of this study along on mission trips to bless the missionaries with whom you serve. Use it as a gift for wives headed into ministry.

- Use as a reference tool. Keep this book on hand and use it to remind other women in ministry that they are not alone. You may also choose to revisit different topics as needed.

Our prayer for you as you complete this study is summarized by Ephesians 1:17-19. We desire that as you get to know God better through this book that you'll lean on the hope to which He has called you, knowing the inheritance that accompanies His calling and realizing that His incomparable power is at work in your life. May your life overflow with all the goodness the Lord has planned for you!

Blessings!

Jennifer Landrith

Rachel Lovingood

if the shoe fits ...

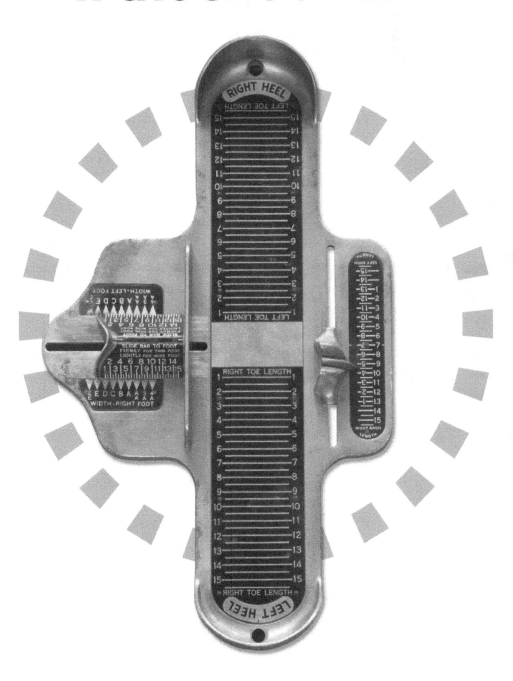

If you love shoes so much that the term "shoe addict" applies to you, you know the frustration that comes when a friend, who is also an ultimate shopper, shows off a new pair of cute shoes and insists that you try them on. With a tentative smile you give her a nod, and so begins the struggle of trying to stuff your size 9 foot into her size 8 heel. Frustration and pain soon result, reminding you that no matter how stylish the footwear, nothing causes discomfort more than shoes that don't fit.

Sometimes we work so hard to make something that isn't right for us "fit." Jeans. Hairstyles. Shoes. But in reality, one style or size rarely fits all. This is particularly true of Bible studies and books geared toward all believers. While truth and great ideas can come from these studies, it's difficult to find one that really addresses the specific concerns of wives in ministry. Nothing beats that feeling of slipping your foot into the softest leather shoe that is just your size. Our hope is that this study will prove a perfect fit for you.

So, where's the best place to start a Bible study for ministry wives? Well, since we come from diverse backgrounds and situations, it's imperative that we focus on what we have in common. Our greatest common denominator is ministry; therefore, it makes sense to start with how we got here.

Let's begin with your calling. Don't stop reading just because you aren't crazy about that term. Remember, the significance of the word is often overlooked because we tend to think about callings in terms of how our husbands decided on their particular jobs, or we think that receiving a calling means receiving a heavenly summons to a specific church or overseas location. The word *calling* applies to all believers, but for the purpose of this chapter we want to focus on the personal, unique calling that wives in ministry need to understand and embrace.

MISSTEP:

If you started this chapter and are tempted to skip through, please be careful not to underestimate the importance of routinely evaluating and confirming your calling. Ask the Lord to open your heart and mind to anything He has to say to you.

The *Holman Bible Dictionary* defines a *calling* as an "invitation, summons, commission, or naming." In our ministry roles, we'll face some very tough times; you may already have experienced some. That's why we as ministers' wives need to recognize and accept God's call on our lives. By remembering the call God has placed on you, you'll find strength to stand when difficulties come.

Which of the following responses best describe your initial answer to God's calling on your life?
- ○ **I'm sorry. I think You have the wrong number.**
- ○ **So glad You called; perfect timing!**
- ○ **Can I get back with You when I'm not so busy?**
- ○ **Good to hear from You! What do You want me to do?**

Read 2 Peter 1:10-11. What does Peter advise you to do about your call?

What do you think he means?

These questions will receive special attention during group time.

When Peter admonished believers to "make their calling sure," he wanted them to confirm in their own hearts just what the Lord had called them to do. How might confirming your call impact your life?

How might it impact your ministry?

Your relationship with your spouse?

If you confirm your calling to serve alongside your spouse here on earth and respond to God's invitation, accepting all He has planned for you, you get the promise of not stumbling (Jude 24). You also get the bonus of a rich welcome into the kingdom of heaven. Think of Paul's assurance in terms of buying a season ticket to one theme park and getting entrance to another. Here in Tennessee when you purchase a special ticket for Dollywood you automatically receive admission to Splash Country. It's a great two-for-one deal.

Making your calling sure is the ultimate two-for-one deal. Amazingly, this gift comes free to all who accept it. Now don't get confused. We aren't talking about salvation here. Instead, we want to focus on the additional calling you receive after choosing to accept Christ as Savior. From this point on in our study, we'll assume you are a follower of Jesus Christ. We realize, however, that not everyone in ministry is saved. Only those who believe in their hearts that Jesus is Lord, confess their sins to Him, and ask His forgiveness belong to God's family and will one day enter heaven. You must first answer God's call to salvation before focusing on God's call on the rest of your life.

Although most ministry wives would agree that some type of divine calling on their lives brought them to this point, they often define it with an adjective placed in front of the word "calling" rather than trying to understand what their callings mean on a personal level. The majority of women we've encountered identify with one of these four descriptions of their calling.

1. A SPECIFIC calling.

Women who connect with this description feel a clear, distinct call to ministry. Some knew they would marry ministers and prepared for that. Some began ministry and then married into ministry, but they all knew that ministry was their calling.

2. A GENERAL calling.

These ladies felt called to serve the Lord and were willing to do so, but they didn't necessarily know the exact direction it would take them. Perhaps they felt called to work with the homeless or maybe even overseas and now serve alongside their husbands in various ministries.

3. An UNEXPECTED calling.

Wives in this category felt surprised by the call to ministry. They may have married accountants who became business pastors or teachers who became youth leaders. While these wives hadn't planned on being in ministry, they accept their new positions willingly.

4. An IMPERSONAL calling.

Women who identify with this description see ministry as their husband's job—an impersonal call that doesn't apply to them. Often they resist the concept of partnering with their husbands in ministry.

> **If you strongly identified with one of these categories, put a star beside it.**

Which of the statements best describes how you view your calling? It's possible that you had a hard time deciding. Remember that the word *calling* refers to an invitation, and God will not force you to accept His invitation or call. Let's have a little fun with this whole concept by comparing the four typical perceptions of God's call to ministry with four different parties to which we as ministry wives might receive invites.

Read the following party descriptions and put a heart beside the one that best relates to your situation.

A Formal Ball

This event is for those wives who excitedly received God's invitation to serve in ministry. Like gorgeously dressed Cinderellas heading to the palace, their response to God's call to serve is always a resounding "Yes, Lord." No matter what difficulties arise, they generally dance through the situation with glass slippers on their feet.

The challenge faced by ball attendees is that their own original callings from the Lord can override any new direction God may send, often leading them to struggle with letting God redirect and reshape their callings as He chooses. For example, we have talked with wives who originally felt called to missions and now find themselves married to children's pastors. Others find themselves home, raising the kids, when they had thought they would serve as the full-time staff person. These women sometimes feel discontented as life forces them to exchange their glass slippers for more useful footwear.

A Progressive Dinner

This get-together is similar to the formal ball in that attendees originally responded to God's invitation with excitement. They felt called to serve the Lord but didn't know exactly how that would play out in their lives. Many of these wives never actually felt called to ministry personally; but because they felt led to marry their husbands, they ended up partnering with them in ministry. Because these ladies trust that God is in charge of all things, they readily and willingly serve in various ways.

The challenge faced by those attending the progressive dinner is to continue to flexibly bend to God's direction even when life feels comfortable. These party-goers need encouragement to remain willing to try new things when tempted to stick with their broken-in favorites.

The Surprise Party

Wives at this party never expected to serve in the ministry. They thought they married businessmen and were then shocked by their husbands' announcements: "Honey, I've been called to preach, teach, or lead within the church." Often with little or no warning, they accepted a call they neither imagined or received formal training to prepare them for it. They're willing to serve but sometimes feel overwhelmed.

The challenge for attendees of this party is to overcome any feelings of insecurity or inadequacy and to adjust to the unexpected changes this calling brings. Though they may sometimes feel as if they've shown up for a formal masquerade in sweats and tennis shoes, they need to relax and let the Lord help them make the best of their current situation.

A Bachelor Party

Wives who received this invitation think of ministry as a bachelor party and feel as if they have no place. They often miss out on what it means to partner with their husbands in doing the work of the Lord. These wives feel the invitation came for their husbands and not for them personally. They look in on ministry from the outside while their husbands have the time of their lives inside. These wives resist becoming involved in ministry because they consider it their husbands' work and not their own.

Those in this group face a unique challenge. While their husbands can tell them about the exciting things happening in the ministry, they can't enjoy ministry as the personal blessing it is designed to be unless they choose to willingly participate.

What about the party description you selected relates to you?

No matter which party description most appealed to you, you can benefit from taking a fresh look at God's calling on your life. Look at the blank invitation and take a few minutes to pray, asking God to reveal to you exactly what He has called you to do. Then complete the card by filling in your name and elaborating on your calling, listing the specific ministry steps God wants *you* to take.

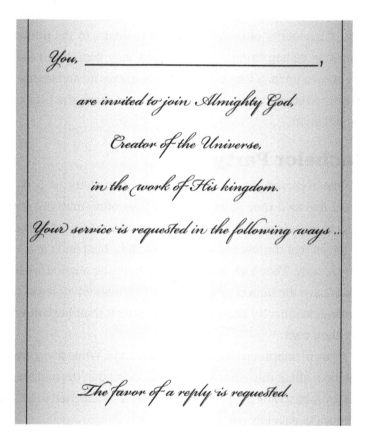

You, _____,

are invited to join Almighty God,

Creator of the Universe,

in the work of His kingdom.

Your service is requested in the following ways ...

The favor of a reply is requested.

If this invitation feels impossible for you to complete with a list of concrete and, yes, enjoyable ways you can participate in ministry, please don't give up! Discouragement may endure for a moment, but God offers hope. Our husbands often remind people that it is easier to act your way into a feeling than to feel your way into an action. This powerful concept can apply to your attitude toward God's calling on your life.

List at least three things to which you are definitely called. For example,

I am called to be <u>the wife of Jeff</u>.

I am called to be <u>the mom of Rachel, Sam and Josh</u>.

I am called to <u>teach 12th grade girls.</u>

1. **I am called to** _____.
2. **I am called to** _____.
3. **I am called to** _____.

No matter how you answered this exercise, the point is clear. The Lord has important plans specifically designed to bless you and the lives of those around you.

Read these verses and write what you discover that relates to your calling as a minister's wife.

Galatians 5:13

1 Corinthians 1:9

1 Peter 2:9

ACTION STEP:

Discuss with your
husband his specific
call to ministry and
how it relates to
you. Share some of
your insights from
this chapter and
talk about ways
that living out your
own ministry calling
can support and
encourage him in his
ministry role.

As Christians and as ministers' wives we've been chosen, called to bring light, to serve, and to fellowship with Jesus! While you continually pray for God to give you a deeper sense of calling to ministry, focus on these things. God will use them to help you better understand and solidify your calling.

God doesn't want us confused about our callings. That's why it's important to recognize that our calling to serve as ministry wives is not static but dynamic; in other words, it may not always stay the same. For instance, a couple called to youth ministry may end up as senior pastor and a pastor and his wife may receive a new call into a chaplaincy or parachurch ministry. God is not the author of confusion, and He wants us to be at peace and content in the calling placed on us and our husbands. Daniel 2:28 says, "There is a God in heaven who reveals mysteries" (HCSB). If your calling is a mystery at this point, don't despair; instead, ask God to bring clarification. In the meantime, continue serving in your usual manner until He makes the fullness of His direction for you more specific. Cling to the commands given to all believers: seek Him, know Him, and keep on loving your neighbors as yourself. As you do, you'll grow increasingly focused on Him and more in tune with the plans He has for you.

First Thessalonians 5:23-24 reminds us that God is faithful to help us live worthy of our calling. When we trust in Him, we'll receive the power to accomplish what He wants to do through us. When we finish with this world and hang up life's shoes, we'll find ourselves in the presence of the Lord. Our hope is that Jesus will one day say to us, "Well done, good and faithful servant. You have served me well and remained blameless and pure so that I could do what I purposed in your life" (Matthew 25:21, author's paraphrase). When you gratefully wear the different ministry shoes God gives you, making the most of every opportunity, then you will position yourself to hear those words!

designer's original

S ome popular Web sites allow shoppers to design their own shoes. Weeks after creating your unique footwear, you'll find a box of designer's originals at your door. While the privilege of designing your own shoes costs quite a bit, some argue that the experience is worth the price.

After all, if you choose your favorite style and color, you're pretty much guaranteed to love the result. This new option indicates the culture is better understanding the fact that one size and style doesn't fit all. As believers who read Scripture, we recognize that God loves variety, too. The Creator designed each of us with a unique identity, and the Lord takes far more pleasure in making us individuals than the most committed designer could ever find in creating a new shoe.

Recognizing and appreciating our identities as God's designer originals affects our success as ministry wives. Consider the importance of identity on this level: Have you ever answered your phone without knowing who has called? If the person on the other end just launched into a conversation, you probably struggled several minutes to figure out who was on the line. Not understanding to whom you are speaking causes confusion. Not understanding who you are causes frustration and insecurity.

In the days before caller ID technology, people dealt with the issue of identifying themselves in different ways. The writers of the New Testament generally began their letters with a type of self-description that let readers know exactly who addressed them. These greetings also established on whose authority their words came.

Write Romans 1:1 below. Underline phrases that Paul used to describe or identify himself.

Our first chapter dealt with the idea that we each possess individual callings. Now our focus moves to identity: who exactly are we in Christ?

As women we fill many different roles and wear many different hats. The good news is that we, like Paul, can know who we are and what God calls us to do.

Circle all the words that describe your current roles.

cook driver maid wife sister friend teacher

counselor advisor room-mom

babysitter accountant team mom

bookkeeper daughter nurse waitress secretary

Along with each role comes a different description of you: "Riley's mom," "David's wife," and "the marketing director." Add to that list "spiritual leader in the church" and you'll easily see why so many ministers' wives face identity crises.

Describe yourself without using the words *daughter*, *wife*, or *mom*.

On the scale, rate how difficult you found this activity.

Very Difficult   **Somewhat Difficult**   **Fairly Easy**   **No problem**

We aren't suggesting that identification as part of a family or group is bad or wrong. Our point is that it's important we each know ourselves should these roles suddenly disappear. Many women become so dependent on the roles of their lives that they struggle with describing themselves in separate terms. Sometimes they even hide behind their different roles to keep people from knowing too much about them.

What about you? Do you ever hide the real you behind your husband's job description or your children's accomplishments?

Circle factors that may influence ministry wives to hide behind a certain role or term. (Add any others that apply.)

	Insecurity	Nervousness
Fear	Confusion	Others' expectations
	Past mistakes	Inadequate training

The failure to present ourselves as capable, unique individuals with relevant opinions and likable traits often comes down to fear. We struggle with questions like, "What if I fail to prove myself a good friend? Will people still like me if they see my weaknesses as well as my strengths? Can people relate to me as a normal person just like them instead of labeling me 'the pastor's wife'?"

Wouldn't the world and the church be less intimidating if people could shamelessly announce their personality quirks right off the bat instead of hiding behind formalities? Maybe, for instance, we could all wear nametags proclaiming things like "Hi, my name is ..., I'm high maintenance ..., I talk a lot ..., I am extremely insecure ..., or I need sympathy."

What would a nametag describing you say? Fill out the sample. Make it fun; this is for your eyes only.

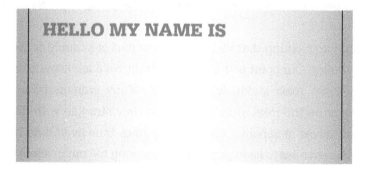

HELLO MY NAME IS

Fortunately, these revealing tags will never be stylish. But while few would agree to introduce themselves with such blunt honesty, we could all benefit from growing more authentic and comfortable with the unique way God made us. When we do, we'll feel more secure in acting as ourselves around new acquaintances and even old friends.

Many times we talk to ministry wives who feel intimidated by the thought of relaxing in their interactions. As a result, many women constantly play the comparison game: "I need to play the piano like Andrea." "If only I dressed as sharply as Janice." "My husband's ministry could be so much better if I were a strong speaker like Julie." This type of thinking is futile and counterproductive. When you choose to compare yourself to others, you invariably come up on the losing end. Why? Because we are all the Designer's originals, created differently to fulfill specific purposes. Remember that you as a ministry wife—and as a woman, for that matter—were created for a purpose that's yours alone. Strive to be the woman God designed you to be, trusting that He knows exactly what He is doing.

Read the following statements, marking each *(T)* for true and *(F)* for false.

___ **God is not surprised that I married a minister.**

___ **God knows me, warts and all.**

___ **God loves me just the way I am.**

___ **God knows the "stuff" I deal with.**

___ **God wants to use me right now.**

___ **God knows what is best for me.**

___ **God knows all about my "junk."**

___ **God forgives and restores me.**

___ **God thoroughly understands how my past affects my present and my future.**

Each statement rings true. Why then, do we often act as if God expects us to live just like someone else who hasn't walked in our shoes and who knows little about our personal stories? The answer is that He wouldn't. He doesn't. And neither should you. Remember, the

MISSTEP:

The comparison game is dangerous. To whom are you tempted to compare yourself?

comparison game can't be won. Understand that the Lord stamped you with this label: "Lovingly and Uniquely Designed by God." Understanding God's claim over our lives as believers helps us overcome the fears and insecurities that make us hesitant to act like ourselves.

When we struggle with self-doubt, we've found that it's encouraging to study some heroes of the faith who experienced similar issues. Throughout Scripture God took very different women with very different problems, personalities, and experiences and used them for His glory and their good.

Rahab, for example, overcame a life of prostitution to become an ancestor of Jesus Christ. Sarah released her determination to do things her own way and discovered that God's way is best. Ruth struggled over devastating personal losses yet found love and acceptance as God's plan for her unfolded. Mary, who faced judgment and humiliation, endured life's struggles to become the mother of Jesus as God worked the greatest miracle in her humble life.

The common denominator linking these women's experiences to our own is that each believed God. They didn't just believe in God's existence; they trusted in God's ability to see them through life's circumstances.

FUN FLIPS:

What characteristics would you include if creating the formula for a perfect minister's wife? Why do you think God chooses not to apply a "perfect formula" of personality traits and abilities to ministry wives?

No mold exists for godly women. No mold exists for ministers' wives. If you began your life as a minister's wife believing you should play the piano, lead all the Bible studies, teach children's Sunday School, and sing in the choir, you need to understand that God expects you to do what He directs you to do—not what others expect.

Later, we will more fully address dealing with unrealistic expectations from people in the church. For now do yourself a favor (and the minister of music a favor if you sing like us) and ask God to show you how He wants you to serve at this season of life. While you may face challenges within that service, remember that His "yoke is easy and [His] burden is light" (Matthew 11:30, NIV).

If you struggle with accepting yourself as the unique individual the Lord created you to be, let us remind you of some things God says about you:

1 Peter 2:10

You are a part of the people of God. You have received mercy.

Ephesians 1:3-4

You are blessed with spiritual blessings. You are chosen.
You are holy and blameless.

Ephesians 2:19

You are a fellow citizen of heaven. You are a member of God's household.

ACTION STEP:

Live secure in who you are in Christ. All over your house—on the mirror, on the fridge, on the computer monitor—post Scripture verses reminding you of your identity in the Lord.

Read the following passages and write what else God says about you:

1 Corinthians 3:16

2 Corinthians 3:3

Colossians 3:12

Wow! Did you catch that last one? You are "Christ's letter," not written with ink but written on the heart! Scripture overflows with good stuff like this that applies to believers, yet so many of us settle for a life of mediocrity that doesn't reflect what we say we believe. We may possess head knowledge of our identity in Christ, but we need to let it transform into heart knowledge that changes the way we live and think about ourselves.

Consider the verses in the last activity. Which statement do you most struggle to believe and claim for your life? Mark that passage with a star.

Understand that false beliefs and unrealistic expectations about ourselves tend to weigh down our walks with the Lord. Thinking of ourselves negatively long enough can lead us toward believing in and acting on those false assumptions. The cool thing is that the opposite is also true. If you act on truth long enough and intentionally enough, then you begin to believe it and it becomes a vital part of your life.

Complete the following prayer with truths stated in the verse(s) you starred.

**Father God,
I know You are with me and that You have great plans for my life. I truly want to believe You for all the things I read about in Your Word. I ask You to help my unbelief about these truths ...**

Help my life reflect what I know to be true about You and me.

We encourage you to do whatever it takes to incorporate scriptural truths about your identity in Christ into your daily life. But remember, settling the issue of who you are right now doesn't mean that the matter is settled forever. As our seasons of life change, the roles we fill in our families and churches evolve. For instance, a stay-at-home mom might begin working part time, and a working mom will eventually become an empty nester.

Although your identity in Christ never changes, your life will always change. Be prepared so that an identity crisis doesn't blindside you. Cling to what God's Word claims about you.

If you are currently experiencing an identity crisis, don't take the "ostrich approach" to your situation. Burying your head in the sand doesn't remove you from difficulty; it just blinds you to nearby help.

Evaluate your life through God's eyes and deal with the hurdles and hang-ups He reveals to you. Some of the following chapters will offer practical suggestions on how to do this, but the key is to believe that God can and will help you with any struggle. He is waiting for you to ask Him.

One last point before we leave this topic. Embracing a healthy identity in Christ requires us to understand that God loves us too much to leave us the way we are.

Unfortunately, some women use the whole "God made me this way" excuse to justify ungodly behavior. This includes everything from insulting people under the justification of a prophetic gift or routinely justifying sin as if doing so illustrates mercy.

True, God made you and wants to use you "warts and all," but He also loves you enough that He wants you to continually grow and serve and love more like Jesus.

We once heard a speaker comment, "I hope if you see me next year you won't even recognize me. I hope that I'll be more like Jesus to the point that I look and act nothing like I do today." Those strong words should reflect the desire of our hearts as we continually change, grow, and develop into the women God designed us to become.

None of us would go online and design our own shoes only to refuse to open the box and wear them upon delivery. We wouldn't

ACTION STEP:

Ask God to increase your sensitivity to areas of your life where you resist allowing Him to change you. As He convicts you of thoughts, actions, or words that are contrary to His Word, actively respond by making a plan of what you specifically will commit to doing in order to change.

complain about them and treat them as worthless. Why? Because we created and designed them just as we wanted for a specific use. In fact, they would likely hold a place of honor in the closet!

It's time to look in the mirror and accept that the Great Designer made you for a specific purpose. You can respond to any identity crisis with the firm conviction that "God never makes mistakes." He has set our feet on this path of ministry—it's up to us to keep walking.

shoes with attitude

Have you ever noticed how you can raise a plain, not so exciting outfit to the next level of fashion simply by adding just the right pair of shoes? Your everyday jeans and plain t-shirt go from casual to chic with a pair of cool plaid wedges. That forgettable black dress makes lasting memories when you add your strappy red heels. And a fun pair of flip-flops paired with a favorite outfit conveys "I'm laid back and relaxed" like nothing else. Letting your shoes make a statement reflects a phenomenon we like to call "shoes with attitude."

The addition of a little "attitude" goes an amazingly long way toward changing a person's entire outlook on a situation. You've probably seen this proven in your own life at times when viewing life's glass as half empty instead of half full becomes your norm. You know, those times when it's easier to complain about your crazy schedule than to celebrate the large numbers of students reached with the gospel during the summer months. Those moments when you want to roll your eyes when someone comments about the wonderful sermon your husband preached because all you can think about is his general orneriness on Mondays. All of us experience moments when negativity takes over, but we need to realize that the attitude we choose speaks volumes.

We've spent time in previous chapters considering our identity in Christ and discussing how we arrived at our current ministry roles. Let's focus now on how to make the most of the positions in which God placed us.

Rate your current attitude toward the church in which you serve.

1	10

I can't stand it.   I'm disappointed in it.   It's OK.   I love it!

So much of our effectiveness as ministry wives, and even as Christians, is influenced by our attitudes. Like a daring pair of shoes that can either elevate an everyday outfit to something extraordinary or lower the perfect ensemble into a fashion disaster, our attitudes will either make or break our opportunities to serve the Lord. That's why we must continually put our best foot, or attitude, forward. Whether we serve in the nursery, lead a Bible Study, or witness to a neighbor; we need to remember that people deserve our best.

Living out the words of Colossians 3:23, which challenges us to do everything as to the Lord, requires that all aspects of our attitudes or viewpoints glorify Him. Considering how your past can influence your present will help you make sure your attitude lines up.

Answer the following questions to evaluate the role your past plays on your current attitude or viewpoint toward ministry.

Did you grow up in a church?   Yes   No

If you answered yes, did you grow up in the same denomination as the one in which you serve now?

If no, describe your introduction into the denomination in which you currently serve.

Which of the following words best describe(s) the church in which you grew up? Circle all that apply.

traditional   formal   turbulent

casual   large   growing   small

charismatic   dull   legalistic

evangelical   rigid   liberal   exciting

conservative   mission-minded   family-oriented

Name three people who have influenced you spiritually. In one sentence, summarize a spiritual discipline each person taught you either in words or by example. (For example: Nancy challenged me to take my prayer life seriously. Dianna knew so much Scripture that I desired to memorize the Word.)

1.

2.

3.

Place a star beside the statement that best describes your situation.

I'm the first person in my family to serve in ministry.

Ministry is part of my family's heritage.

My family was involved in the lay aspect of church.

Church was never a part of my childhood background.

Which of the following best describes your family's view of people in ministry?

Ministry is for people who couldn't get any other job.

Ministers deserve obedience and respect in all circumstances.

Ministers are God's anointed and need our prayers and support.

Ministers are lazy. Who else gets to work one day a week?

We've discovered that a woman's church background often impacts her overall attitude toward the call to serve as a ministry wife. Many of us grew up in churches with traditions emphasized to the point that they seemed to be scriptural mandates rather than just local customs of a particular church.

For instance, we might struggle with the thought of wearing jeans on Sunday morning. Certainly no Bible verse speaks against denim in the house of God. But at the church we grew up in dresses—not jeans—belonged in church on Sunday mornings. To this day we sometimes pause at the thought of wearing jeans to Sunday morning worship. While you may laugh or roll your eyes at this example, you can probably think of some similar hang-ups in your life.

We need to recognize that times and fashions change, and what works in one geographic locale may not float in the next. (For instance, if you move to a beach community, you might wear flip-flops to church at Christmas.) Just as that old adage "no white shoes before Easter or after Labor Day" is quickly slipping into memory, traditions and customs continue to evolve according to the times and places in which we live. This means that unless an idea is scripturally mandated—like participation in the Lord's Supper (1 Corinthians 11:23-26) or baptism

(Matthew 28:19) then you should ask yourself, Would letting go of this tradition help me reach more people with the gospel?

Consider, for instance, if you can relax enough to wear jeans to church for a special event, you may help create an atmosphere where lost people—many of whom don't have dress clothes—may feel more welcome. Likewise, getting hung up on how a church does music or arranges its weekly schedule is not important. Our focus needs to revolve around the question, "What can God most effectively use in our particular area of the country?" Sometimes the answer requires that we lay aside our preferences.

At our church we always say that we will never change the message of the gospel; our methods, however, remain open to change to help people find Christ. This motto easily applies to our personal interactions. Remember, relaxing traditions and preferences so that we can focus more on the things Christ really expects of us helps us become more like Him.

Paul weighed in on this topic in his letter to the Corinthian church.

Paraphrase 1 Corinthians 9:22.

How does this concept impact the issues we've been considering?

The example Paul gives us of his willingness to lay aside some pretty strong beliefs and traditions to reach lost people should challenge and motivate us. After all, Paul dealt with bigger cultural strongholds than jeans, personal pews, dresses, makeup and the appropriateness of pantsuits.

Name a tradition you struggle to release.

How might refusing to change hinder your effectiveness in bringing others to Christ?

Don't take our stance against stronghold traditions to mean that past church experiences can't positively influence viewpoints. Without a doubt, growing up in church is wonderful; and the fellowships where we first learned biblical truths may help us develop a love for evangelism or foster a strong desire to help those less fortunate.

In many cases, early experiences in church lay the foundation of our relationships with Christ. Unfortunately, however, some personal church experiences do leave people dealing with subtle unspoken messages that can trip them as they strive to grow in the Lord. These things seldom stem from a part of the church's mission statement or even from something broadcast from the pulpit.

Maybe, for example, you grew up in a church that used a person's decision to go forward to the altar as fuel for its gossip chain. Perhaps your church's leadership was notorious for sweeping any major mistakes under the rug of pride instead of dealing with them in an open, biblical fashion. You may even struggle with hard feelings toward church because your particular congregation took an unbiblical approach toward a pregnant teen or even encouraged an adulterous relationship between its members.

FUN FLIPS:

Occasional struggles with hard feelings toward church are common, but they shouldn't control us. List three surefire ways you can brighten your attitude (i.e. shoe shopping, indulging in chocolate, taking a bubble bath)

Rate your attitude toward church in general.

1	10

I can't stand it.   I'm disappointed in it.   It's OK.   I love it!

Each of us is influenced by our past, but God gives us the option of deciding whether to let the past make us bitter or to find blessing in spite of it. Don't misunderstand: life hurts, lacks fairness, and sometimes deals harsh blows. You may have dealt with abuse, adultery, desertion, cancer, death, disillusionment, or any other major trauma, but none of it has to define your life with Christ. We don't mean to downplay your hurt, but we want you to understand that life's negatives don't have the right to steal your joy and fill you with bitterness.

What do the following verses reveal about bitterness?

Proverbs 14:10

Acts 8:23

Hebrews 12:15

To you, what is the worst thing about bitterness?

When are you most tempted to respond with bitterness? Check all that apply.

- ○ **When your husband cancels plans.**
- ○ **When church emergencies interrupt family time.**
- ○ **When your husband is always last to leave the church and gets home late.**
- ○ **When you get another piece of unsolicited advice.**
- ○ **When the yard gets neglected another week.**
- ○ **When the phone never stops ringing.**

MISSTEP:

If you recognize signs of bitterness in your life, deal with them immediately. Don't bury your feelings or ignore them; they won't just disappear. Bitterness left untreated develops deep roots that impact every area of life. Seek counseling and ask God to heal you.

So how do we deal with bitterness? What can we do to walk free of its pull? In Philippians 3:15 Paul encourages believers to press on toward the goal of becoming more mature in their attitudes toward Christ. That type of maturity leads people to intentionally choose blessings over bitterness.

Spiritual growth is difficult to measure. Write the date you became a believer. Draw a growth chart up from the line that depicts your level of spiritual maturity. Include major milestones.

Date I trusted Christ _____

Are you pleased with the description you circled? Does it reflect where you want to stand in your walk with Christ? Paul assures us in Philippians 3:15 that God will reveal any attitudes contrary to a positive outlook focused on Jesus. That means He will help us to recognize things in our lives that take our minds and hearts off Him.

Take a moment and ask God to reveal to you anything that needs to change so that you can continue to mature spiritually. Use this space to record the insights you receive.

As we've sought to grow in the Lord, we've learned to focus not on past church experiences that hurt us or even current ones that frustrate. Some of our favorite blessings from ministry come when we read e-mails of how peoples' lives have been changed by God as a result of our church's ministry or when ladies in the church share how the Holy Spirit restored their marriages after adultery.

We've come to realize that serving in ministry is all about being a part of something that is bigger than us. It's about serving a God who does great and mighty things regardless of our pasts. We've compiled a list of specific blessings that remind us why it's a privilege to serve as ministry wives:

- Sometimes the Holy Spirit's work in our church and in our families is so powerful we can hardly breathe.
- We get the joy of seeing God's hand at work in others' lives.

- The opportunities to share or minister are multiplied through our church involvement.
- We get to know behind-the-scenes details regarding how God brings everything together in spite of people.
- We get to spend time with people who genuinely love God.
- We can watch people grow into mature believers.
- We see lives change, marriages heal, and prodigal children come home.
- We're among the first to receive updates when God answers prayers.
- Our close church involvement gives us built-in accountability by responsibility that helps us keep our spiritual lives on track.
- The joy of raising our families in church is a perk.
- People take special interest in our kids.
- We enjoy built-in, extended families.
- When we move, we don't have to look for a new church home.

What blessings can you add to this list?

ACTION STEP:
Write out an abbreviated copy of the list on pages 38-39. Keep it handy, allowing it to encourage you to choose an attitude of blessing when negativity threatens.

Don't misunderstand and think us clueless about the very real struggles involved in ministry life. We know service within a local church is difficult and can feel like you're running a sprint in four-inch heels. We will discuss some of these issues specifically in other chapters, but first we must realize while we can't control all the negative things that come our way, we can control our response to them.

The beloved fictional character, Pollyanna, gives us a hint on how to approach life with a positive outlook. She could find joy in the most

ACTION STEP:

Share Psalms 103:1-2 with your family. Challenge them to describe positive moments they've experienced as a result of ministry involvement. Work together to make a "blessing jar" or box. Use it as a container for pieces of paper on which you each write ministry-related blessings. You may choose to read the blessings aloud at your ministry anniversary or as an encouragement when you face tough times as a family.

negative situations, and people delighted in bringing their difficulties to her so that she could find the good in them. Scripture is filled with the stories of people who faced uncertain and even negative circumstances which, when viewed through eyes focused on the Lord, didn't seem so overwhelming. Psalm 61 provides a perfect example of how a struggling person can take his worries to the Lord and find his attitude transformed into one of praise and worship. God's powerful Word can transform the bleakest soul.

Write Psalm 103:1-2 here.

How can these verses help you regularly choose blessings over bitterness?

Psalm 103 presents a great challenge! We must never forget the benefits that come with living lives of true worship and gratitude to the Father. Today you can choose to put on grumbling old work boots and stomp your way around, or you can choose to put on the sparkly shoes of gratitude. If you allow the Lord control over your attitude, everyone will notice and your day can change from "Good Lord, it's morning" to "Good morning, Lord." Your witness of godly living will make a stronger statement than the coolest pair of trendy leather boots.

cross trainers

If someone asked you what type of shoe best symbolizes the life of a ministry wife, you probably wouldn't respond with "stilettos" or "ballet slippers." Undoubtedly, the shoe that most accurately describes the lives of women in ministry is the cross trainer: active footwear meant to keep up with anything that comes a busy woman's way. Cross trainers are supportive, flexible, and ready to run to the school, church, store, gym or ballpark.

The name *cross-trainer* lends important insight into the spiritual goal ministry wives should strive to reach. As we raise our children and encourage members of our churches in their walks with the Lord, we can't neglect our own spiritual training.

So often we as wives, mothers, friends, and workers place ourselves last in everything. We give our husbands priority; we put the church calendar's importance above our own; and the needs of our families and churches consume our days. We've got to understand that while balancing the needs of others with our desire to serve God is tough, we must give our personal relationship with the Lord top priority. God wants us to live as cross-trainers. That means we should place just as much emphasis on tending our own spiritual health as we place on nurturing others'.

When a flight attendant shares the airplane safety procedures, he or she demonstrates how to use the oxygen masks correctly. The attendant always reminds people traveling with small children or those in need of assistance to place the oxygen mask on their own faces first before helping others. Why? Without proper oxygen, even the most devoted person grows listless and unable to help.

The same idea applies to our spiritual oxygen intake. We can't help others unless we first anchor ourselves to the strength-giving flow of God's Spirit in our lives.

Have you ever felt like you were so busy putting everyone else's oxygen mask on that you were at risk of passing out yourself? List the names of those you currently watch over.

Why does your spiritual health really need to be a priority?

You may wonder, Why feel concerned about my spiritual health as long as the ministry is still happening? or Does my personal walk really matter as long as our ministry grows? One temptation for people in our positions is to substitute ministry for personal growth; that is a recipe for disaster. Before you give in to this kind of thinking, consider why you should take your spiritual health seriously.

1. God desires fellowship. The Lord created us for relationship. By developing our spiritual walks, we fulfill one of our main purposes in life.

According to Matthew 6:33, what happens when you put God first and focus on a relationship with Him?

- ○ **Your closets get organized.**
- ○ **God takes care of your needs.**
- ○ **You no longer need to exercise.**
- ○ **Everything in life works out without problems.**

MISSTEP: Allowing ministry to take the place of personal growth can prove disastrous. Are you guilty of substituting ministry for growth in any way? How can you prevent this from happening to you?

When we place God first in our lives, our priorities align, making us better able to live the abundant life described in John 10:10. In our own lives, we've discovered that personal time with the Lord helps us find the answers we need. When the stresses and questions of life come, seek answers from the One directly able to see the big picture. God knows the paths you need to take, and He wants you to ask Him for direction.

How often do you spend time alone with the Lord?

Daily	Every Now and Then	Weekly	Seldom	Never

Along with the benefit of reconnecting your heart to God comes a bonus, a chance to find relief from the multitudes (or at least a break from the kids, the neighbors, the women's group, and, yes, even your husband). So many times we feel we must sacrifice our personal time for the pressing needs of our lives, but we should never feel guilty about spending time alone with God. Jesus Himself continually found time away from the crowds to be alone with the Father (Matthew 14:23) These times fueled Him to complete the ministry opportunities He faced. Get alone with God and let Him refresh and refuel you before you take on life's next hurdle.

2. Scripture makes spiritual health a priority. God cares so much about our spiritual state that He included in Scripture some very clear commands of what we as believers should do. Deuteronomy 6:5 provides an important example.

Read Deuteronomy 6:5 aloud.

> **Summarize Matthew 22:37-39. This passage restates the command given in Deuteronomy and then refers to it as the "greatest and most important commandment." Why do you think Jesus gave this distinction?**

These verses should serve as the motivation behind our commitment to spiritual growth. In our immature, weak, fleshly natures, we can't love God the way He desires; doing so is a maturing process. Our efforts, then, should not stop at obeying God's command. We've got to reach the point that our love for Him grows so strong that disobedience is not an option. God wants your relationship with Him to flourish. Don't offer Him your leftovers. Give Him your best.

Can you honestly say that you love God with all of your heart?   Yes_____   No_____   I'm Not Sure._____

What or who strives to prevent you from loving Him wholeheartedly?

3. Heart-condition affects the ministry. Every husband in service to the church finds his ministry greatly impacted by his wife's spiritual well-being. Our interactions with others reflect the condition of our spiritual states and will either help or hinder people in their walks with God. Humbling thought. Serious challenge.

Read Galatians 5:13. What do you think Paul meant by *called?*

What warning does Paul give?

Understand that we as Christians are free in Christ, but along with that freedom comes responsibility. As ministry wives, we can't adopt attitudes that scream, "I've already given up everything to be in ministry, so I'm entitled to pout and complain." We've got to realize that when we grumble and whine, everything from our marriage relationships to our carpools, to the ministries of our churches suffers.

Although none of us intentionally plans to push aside our spiritual health, it can get overlooked in busyness. We find it easy to neglect our spiritual lives, often reasoning, "Who can tell? I attend every Sunday, and I'm not as bad as so-and-so." We've got to remember that no one is long fooled when a woman's relationship with God moves to the back burner. One speaker explained it this way:

Miss one day of your quiet time, and only you and God know.
Miss two days of your quiet time, and your family knows.
Miss three days of your quiet time, and everyone knows.

FUN FLIPS:

Identify your perfect quiet time routine and setting. How can you turn that ideal into reality?

Spiritual health matters! Fill out the following review to keep the top three reasons we've covered fresh in your mind.
1. **God desires** _____ .
2. _____ **makes spiritual health a** _____ .
3. **Heart** _____ **affects the** _____ .

Each of us needs to develop a deeper relationship with the Lord. But while this growing bond plays a crucial role in the life of every believer, we think it literally defines success for those in active ministry. We can't give our walks with Christ a little attention; they require focused attention.

Which of these distract you from regularly growing in the Lord?

Church events   Television   Husband

Children   Hobbies

Household tension   Sin   Community outreach

Laziness   Work

As you answered that last question, you probably realized that more than "sin" and "laziness" separate us from pursuing more of God. A speaker at our church once said, "Good is the enemy of best." This statement really hit home with us because we realized that although we are involved in many good things at church and in the community, we sometimes allow those good things to war with the best things God wants for us. Sometimes we trade spending time with Him for ministry-related activities about Him. Sometimes we let our personal spiritual growth fall by the wayside while we pour out and invest in others. In these cases we lose ground in the war between good and best.

Ephesians 5:18 says we should "be filled with the [Holy] Spirit." This is vital to keeping our relationships with God and others healthy. It describes the "best" God desires for us. When we are filled with the Spirit, our lives produce fruit: love, joy, peace, patience, kindness, goodness, faithfulness, gentleness, and self-control (Galatians 5:22-23). These traits indicate a healthy spiritual state and they also serve to strengthen us in our interactions with others.

Think of your life as this empty glass. Draw a line to represent your present level of filling with the Holy Spirit. It might help to ask, "How much of my life is surrendered to the Spirit's control?"

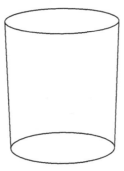

Romans 15:13 states, "Now may the God of hope fill you with all joy and peace in believing, so that you may overflow with hope by the power of the Holy Spirit" (HCSB). This is exciting! If we let God fill our lives, we receive not just what we need but can actually overflow with the Holy Spirit.

Circle five adjectives that best describe you.

Joyful Frustrated Loving Compassionate Stressed
Faithful   Tired   Peaceful   Contented
Patient Disciplined Fragile Spiritually hungry
Kind   Truthful   Frazzled   Discerning
Teachable   Questioning   Creative   Weary

How well do the adjectives you circled match up with the adjectives that should characterize the life of a Spirit-filled believer? (see Galatians 5)

We debated even asking these questions because Satan seeks to para-lyze us with a focus on ourselves. So while we need to practice healthy self-examination, our goal is not for us to feel condemnation but for us to set some realistic goals that will enable us to live spirit filled lives. None of us have it all together, we're all struggling.

Allowing God to fill our busy lives with His Holy Spirit's power is so important! When full of anger, anxiety, and frustration, we have only anger, anxiety, and frustration to offer needy people who cross our paths. However, when we're full of the Holy Spirit, we can offer the life-changing, resurrecting power of God who makes all the difference.

When we want a refreshing drink of diet coke, and we often do, the glass can't already be half filled with milk. Similarly, if we want our lives filled with the Spirit, then we need to consider what we're currently allowing into life's glass. Sometimes the things that hold us back from experiencing the Spirit-filled life are summed up by the word "busyness," but often we allow negative thoughts, idle conversation, and selfish desires to take the place of God's best.

Consider negative things you allow into your life. What keeps you from experiencing an overflow of the Holy Spirit's power?

In the following activity, draw a line from the words that identify your struggles to the inside of the glass. Beside the glass write in any issues we didn't include.

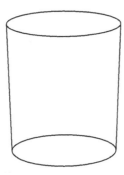

Inappropriate music   Self-Pity   Lust

Inappropriate movies   Internet   Television   Jealousy

Immoral books   Gossip   Vanity   Pride

"Garbage in, garbage out." If we allow jealousy, inappropriate read-ing material, and ungodly thoughts to fill our hearts, we'll soon find ourselves pouring negativity and bad habits on to others. Even more disturbing, we'll miss out on the incredible gift of "Spirit in, Spirit out"—the natural overflow of love and kindness that occurs when we allow God first place in our lives.

Replacing the negative things in our lives with the Holy Spirit's influence is an intentional discipline that brings amazing transformation. We've found that one of the best ways to accomplish this transformation is to use Scripture to "pray off" ungodly attitudes or actions and to "pray on" the things that make us more like Jesus. For instance, we can find a verse that addresses a positive characteristic we need to "put on," pray-ing it for ourselves and committing to change.

Identify characteristics you need to remove to become more like Christ. Then consider what godly characteristic could replace each negative one. For example, if you struggle with a critical spirit, you might use Galatians 5:15 as a starting point to praying a critical nature off your life and then pray on kindness using Colossians 3:12.

Match the following list of negative characteristics with their opposite positive replacements. Use your concord-ance to find verses for any issue not on this list.

Worry/fear	**Forgiving Spirit**
(Philippians 4:6)	*(Colossians 3:13)*
Unforgiving Spirit	**Self-Control**
(Mark 11:26)	*(Galatians 5:22-23)*
Complaining	**Peace**
(Ephesians 4:29)	*(Proverbs 14:30a)*
Strife/Contention	**Contentment**
(Proverbs 13:10)	*(Hebrews 13:5)*
Anger	**Trust**
(Ephesians 4:31)	*(1 Peter 5:7)*
Discontentment	**Praise**
(Hebrews 13:5)	*(Hebrews 13:15)*

Remember, true transformation reaches all areas of our lives. If we are to accept the Holy Spirit's influence, we need to let Him rule the way we think about everything—including ourselves. Scripture says we should love the Lord with all that we are. That seems challenging for those of us who struggle with knowing and understanding ourselves, but we shouldn't allow it to discourage us.

Use the following questions to gain perspective on any areas in which you might not allow God full reign. Place a star beside any question to which you mentally answer in a way contrary to God's desires.

Physical
    ___ Is my body as healthy as I can make it?
    ___ Do I get proper exercise?
    ___ Do I eat right?
    ___ Do I get the rest I need?
    ___ Do I dress modestly?

Emotional
    ___ Do I maintain control over my emotions?
    ___ Do I overreact easily?
    ___ Do I lose my temper often?

___ Do my words reflect the Lord or my sin nature?

___ Do I allow insecurity or jealousy cloud my judgment?

Mental

___ Is the Holy Spirit in control of my thoughts?

___ Do I focus on the negative or positive?

___ Do I do things to increase my knowledge or creativity?

___ Do I seek things that challenge me?

Spiritual

___ Do I regularly spend time alone with God in prayer?

___ Do I seek out and take advantage of witnessing opportunities?

___ Do I routinely study Scripture?

___ Do I have a set time and place to meet with the Lord?

___ Am I committed to putting God's Word in my heart through memorization?

___ Do I set and achieve annual spiritual goals?

Consider the questions you marked with stars. How can you use the insights you gained about yourself to change and strengthen your relationship with God?

With others?

Read 1 Timothy 4:7b-8. In this fitness-crazed world, a focus on physical health seems natural. However, while physical upkeep has merit, Scripture says something else has greater value. What proves more valuable than exercise?

ACTION STEP:
Consider the things you crave. Choose the top three things you want to crave spiritually. Daily pray to desire them.

If you've ever worked to become physically fit, you know just the thought that something's off limits makes the desire to have it overpowering. But what we crave doesn't necessarily align with what we need. Just as we might covertly eat a chocolate bar when our bodies need carrot sticks and peanuts, many people cling to unhealthy behaviors, attitudes, and negative perceptions of self instead of reaching for God's best. First Peter 2:1-2 tells believers to crave "spiritual milk," or the things of the Spirit. That means we should constantly hunger for better understanding of God's Word and closer relationship with Him.

If we want to live in the fullness God offers us as believers, we should adopt the psalmist's heart. No Scripture convicts us, who admittedly fall short of serving God with wholeheartedness, more than Psalm 63. We need to passionately crave God above everything else:

"O God, you are my God,
earnestly I seek you;
my soul thirsts for you,
my body longs for you,
in a dry and weary land
where there is no water." *Psalm 63:1*.

Do you crave the Lord's companionship? Do you long for Him? No matter how you answer, start praying that God will grow you into a true cross trainer who earnestly seeks His best. Our world is a dry and weary land that desperately needs the living Water that only God's followers can share. Be filled with His Spirit and give it away!

double knotted

No one knows how the cliché "tie the knot" came to refer to wedding ceremonies. If you've ever struggled to put on your shoes in a hurry only to find the laces knotted, you can probably make some applications between that experience and marriage. Consider, for example, that although knots are sometimes frustrating to untie, they serve the important purpose of keeping our shoes on our feet. Likewise, the knot of marriage tightens and secures the relationships between our spouses and us. What can at times cause frustration also brings great joy and fulfillment.

Except for the fact that between us we have 40 years of marriage to men in the ministry, we feel extremely ill-equipped to write about this subject. But because certain unique challenges apply to wives in ministry that other wives don't face, we can't skip over this topic just because it's too difficult or we feel unqualified.

Understand that we don't want to suggest that our marriages are perfect, although that would be nice; instead, we want to use this chapter to point out some things we've learned and observed about marriage that can help strengthen all our relationships.

When we hear about friends in the ministry who experience marital troubles, our hearts break and we wonder, How did it get to that point? Was this tragedy preventable? Did the wife try to find help or answers only to be told to try harder, to pray more, and to put on a good face so that no one would know that her marriage was spinning out of control?

Sadly, many couples in ministry are hurting and don't know where to turn. We pray that you learn to proactively invest in your marriage before things get to a crisis point. We want to encourage you to know you are not alone in your frustrations. No matter how discouraging things may seem, the Lord wants you to have a healthy, godly, enjoyable marriage.

How would you rate the strength of your marriage relationship?

1	10	20
We're barely holding it together.	Things could be better.	It's stronger than ever.

Consider a marriage that you would label "healthy" or "ideal." What traits characterize this particular marriage?

As you think about healthy marriages, do you list "lack of conflict" as a sign of strength? We used to think that spouses who never argued enjoyed stronger relationships than ours because we still experience conflict in our homes.

We had to reevaluate our assumptions about healthy marriages when we heard the shocking news that one such couple, who seemingly had it all together, was suddenly dealing with the after-effects of an affair. We began to focus not on what's wrong with problem marriages but rather on what factors help a marriage thrive and not just survive.

When you want to grow physically healthy and strong you perform certain actions and commit to disciplines such as exercise, eating right, and getting the proper amount of rest. These same principles apply to growing and maintaining a strong marriage. By committing to the following three steps, you can strengthen and prepare your relationship to withstand tough times.

1. Let Go of the Bitterness.

If you read that step and thought, Bitter? Who, me? don't tune out. We've found that many women go into marriage to ministers unprepared for the demands ministry makes on their husband's time. Sometimes they even begin to look at the church as "the other woman" in their husband's life. It's not uncommon, in fact, for ministry wives to sometimes feel displaced by the churches in which their husbands serve.

Even seasoned ministry wives face church-related situations that can lead to frustration and dissatisfaction. Perhaps, for instance, hard feelings toward church members and staff persons who don't treat their spouses kindly begin to grow. Sometimes tension evolves between staff wives because of issues involving their husbands. Any situation that brings bitterness into your life can cause damage to your marriage.

Use the following questions to determine whether bitterness poses a threat to you. Underline your answers.

Do you resent the fact that the church and its people are important to your husband?
a. Not really; they do pay his salary.
b. Sometimes, depending on the person ...
c. No, I know he loves me, even if he's focused on someone else.
d. Yes, I am his wife; he better remember it!

Which best describes your Sunday morning attitude?
 a. **Help! I feel like a single mom!**
 b. **If I have to hear him preach on being godly, I'd rather work in the nursery.**
 c. **Thank You, Lord, for another day of worship!**
 d. **Maybe if I look busy no one will talk to me.**

How do you respond when ministry life grows especially demanding?
 a. **I throw a pity party.**
 b. **I complain to whoever will listen.**
 c. **I get on my knees; God is in control!**
 d. **I toughen up and wait it out; I can survive anything.**

Unless you chose option C in response to each of the questions, chances are you sometimes fight the bitterness blahs. But you aren't alone; we've been there too! Over the years we've found a helpful way to deal with bitter feelings the moment they start to threaten: we remind ourselves what God's Word says about them.

Look up the following passages, then draw a line matching each to its related teaching.

Galatians 5:19-21   Put away all bitterness and rage.
                           Forgive as God forgives.

Ephesians 4:31-32   Jealousy or envy rots to the bones.

                           People who choose the things
                           of the flesh will not inherit the
Proverbs 14:30   kingdom of God.

Proverbs 14:30 warns that envy or jealousy (depending on your trans-
lation) will rot or eat you up with decay—not a pretty picture. Bitter
feelings can start with wishful thinking like this. We wish our husbands
had normal jobs. We wish Sundays were the relaxing adventures seemingly enjoyed by our neighbors. We wish people would just leave us
alone, letting us live without their input. These thoughts point to the
reality that we sometimes envy the lives lived by others instead of
appreciating the ones God planned for us.

If you want to live free of the spiritual rot discontentment brings,
turn your frustrations over to the Lord. He can help you choose to see
life's aggravations as blessings. When we allow Christ to transform our
attitudes towards our husbands' work and toward the individuals who
make up our churches, people notice—more importantly, our husbands
will notice and our marriages will be dramatically impacted.

**Do you tend to approach life with an attitude more of
bitterness or blessing? Circle your answer.**

**Would your husband say your general attitude is more
bitter or blessed?**
Bitter   Blessed   Why?

**If you answered that last question with "bitter," what
will you do to change his perception?**

2. Accept the Realities of His Job

Another factor at war against the health of our marriages is the tension
that comes when our husbands must sometimes put church business
ahead of family time. The truth is that our men have jobs to do that
involve people with ever-changing needs; we can't demand all our
husbands' attention.

We find it helps to remember that we can enjoy our husbands'
company when other people can't. With that in mind, we try to strike

a balance between being involved with the ministry and letting them go do ministry. Sometimes separating the work aspects of church from home life helps keep our attitudes healthy when we face the stress of a lengthy revival, building campaign, youth camp, or other special focus times. Different seasons of church life require different measures of grace between us and our spouses; no matter the circumstances, we try to give grace and forgiveness as we've received it—easier said than done sometimes!

Read the following scenarios and choose the responses that best summarize your typical reactions.

Your husband goes on a mission trip, and you must take the annual Spring Break trip to the beach with your parents instead of him. Your son continually asks "Why isn't Daddy here?" You look him in the eye and answer ...

○ **Daddy who?**
○ **Honey, Daddy took the teenagers to share Jesus with people, so we need to remember to pray for them all.**
○ **He's at work, as usual.**
○ **Aren't you having fun with Mommy?**

Your husband feels the Lord wants him to donate your new car savings to the church building fund. You ...

○ **agree with his decision, silently praying that God will somehow work it out.**
○ **get mad and resort to the silent treatment, refusing intimacy until he gets a car.**
○ **accept that you will keep your car longer, pray it doesn't die, and ask the Lord to give your husband wisdom.**

Although other factors affect our success as couples, routine maintenance of our marriage relationships proves vitally important to balancing marriage and ministry. Dr. Adrian Rogers often taught that ministry couples should commit to the three D's: Dialogue daily, date weekly and depart quarterly. Following these practices can prevent you from losing your marriage identity in the midst of the ministry.

Out of our own determination to balance the realities of our husbands' jobs with home life we've compiled the following list of tips to ministry-marriage success. Read through the list, placing a checkmark by your favorite.

• **See the big picture.** Remember that service in ministry is a privilege. People's lives change for eternity because of what you and your husband do.

• **Be flexible.** Learn to fill out your calendar in pencil and not permanent marker. Don't moan when your schedule gets messed up because a funeral shortens your family vacation time or a wedding lands on your child's birthday. Choose to adjust with a smile and a prayer.

• **Don't take it personally.** Try not to place your husband in the position of having to choose between you and his responsibilities. Ministry is not a 9 to 5 job; it never will be.

• **Be smart about timing your conversations.** Pick the right time to chat with your spouse about heavy things or big discussions. One pastor described Monday mornings as a "Holy Hangover," which is a great illustration of what happens when our husbands emotionally and spiritually empty themselves to the point of exhaustion. Remaining sensitive to your husband's emotional needs will strengthen your ability to communicate effectively.

- **Don't cry wolf.** Respect the ministry and the fact that the way your husband conducts himself directly impacts how people perceive those in full or part-time church service. Don't take advantage of your husband's more flexible work schedule by calling him home in the middle of the day to watch the kids so you can get a haircut. Allow him the freedom to do his job; and when you have an emergency, ask him to adjust his schedule.

- **Guard your thoughts.** Don't assume that your husband doesn't love you or think you important just because he couldn't make it home for dinner. Try not to condemn his actions before giving him a chance to explain what happened. Never think the worst. Second Corinthians 10:5 addresses this issue by reminding us to take every thought captive to Christ Jesus.

- **Recognize the positives.** Thank God for all the perks of being married to your man. Your behind-the-scenes knowledge of his strengths and weaknesses should remind you of God's awesome power as He uses human frailty to accomplish His work.

FUN FLIPS:
List things you really like and appreciate about your husband. Take time to let him know how you feel, affirming him for the positives. Be creative!

- **Pray without ceasing.** Maintain an attitude of prayer about your husband. When he calls with a change or issue, go to God. Stormie Omartian's book *The Power of a Praying Wife* provides a great way to organize your prayer efforts for your mate.

- **Remember the wisdom of Philippians 4:8.** Recite this verse and use it to remind yourself to keep the positives in the forefront of life and marriage: "Whatever is true, whatever is noble, whatever is right, whatever is pure, whatever is lovely, whatever is admirable—if anything is excellent or praiseworthy—think about such things."

Which of the tips did you check? How can you put it into practice this week?

3. Meet His Needs

Obviously no chapter on marriage is complete without talking about the "s" word. No, not submission. Sex. This issue needs addressing because it can and often does create real problems in marriages. In fact, many women with otherwise healthy marriages admit struggling with this subject.

In the book *His Needs/Her Needs*, Dr. Willard Harley lists the top five marriage relationship needs of both women and men. After interviewing thousands of couples during his twenty-five years as a marriage counselor, he developed this list:

Men	**Women**
1. Sex	1. Affection
2. Recreational Companionship	2. Communication
3. Attractive spouse	3. Honesty and openness
4. Domestic Support	4. Financial support
5. Admiration	5. Family Commitment

What's surprising about these two lists?

Do these lists reflect you and your husband? If you disagree, ask your spouse what he would list as his top relationship needs.

Notice number one on the men's list? Sex. What doesn't even make the top five on the women's list? Sex. If not for the fact that we can trust that God knows what He's doing, we might question the wisdom of making the genders with such different lists of marital needs. But understand that the Lord created husbands and wives to complement each other, both in the bedroom and outside it.

With God's help, even the most frustrating marital challenges can give way to a great marriage. Keep that in mind and let's see what Scripture says about sex and marriage. Before we do, understand that God did not intend these verses as a weapon against you or for condemnation. He gives these directives as loving instructions from a wise Creator to His beloved creations.

Read First Corinthians 7:4-5.
Does it bother you that your body is not your own? Why or why not?

Why do you think God instructs husbands and wives to not withhold physical love from one another?

What can happen when we deprive our mates of sexual activity? (v. 5b)

Read through Ephesians 5:22-33. Underline all the specific instructions for wives.

Wives, submit to your own husbands as to the Lord, for the husband is head of the wife as also Christ is head of the church. He is the Savior of the body. Now as the church submits to Christ, so wives should [submit] to their husbands in everything. Husbands, love your wives, just as also Christ loved the church and gave Himself for her, to make her holy, cleansing her in the washing of water by the word. He did this to present the church to Himself in splendor, without spot or wrinkle or any such thing, but holy and blameless. In the same way, husbands should love their wives as their own bodies. He who loves his wife loves himself. For no one ever hates his own flesh, but provides and cares for it, just as Christ does for the church, since we are members of His body. For this reason a man will leave his father and mother and be joined to his wife, and the two will become one flesh. This mystery is profound, but I am talking about Christ and the church. To sum up, each one of you is to love his wife as himself, and the wife is to respect her husband (Ephesians 5:22-33, HCSB).

Notice that we didn't ask you to focus on what your husband is supposed to do but on your responsibilities as a wife. This passage is not written as an "If/Then" statement. You can't read it as "If your husband treats you right, then you need to ..." Scripture asks us to lovingly submit to our husbands as unto the Lord. When God makes a request, we need to obey. He created sex not just for the purpose of procreation, but so that husbands and wives could bond together as one. For that reason, sex should be a priority in marriage.

Choosing to disregard the teaching of the Bible is sin. Ignoring what Scripture has to say on this particular subject can have a devastating impact on the quality of your marriage. Why? Because turning our backs on what God has to say about our relationships with our spouses is essentially choosing to leave Him out of our marriages. Most of us need all the help we can get.

Read Ecclesiastes 4:12.
Who is the "third strand" in a godly marriage?

Only when we allow God His rightful place in our lives are our marriages strong and sound.

To help identify whether or not you're allowing God His place in your married life, mark the following statements *(T)* for true and *(F)* for false.

_____ I try to manipulate my husband into things I think he should do.

_____ I pray for the Lord to reveal things to my spouse instead of nagging him about them.

_____ I always have to get in the last word.

_____ I pout and give the silent treatment when my husband doesn't see things my way.

_____ When we disagree, I defer to my husband's judgment and pray for our unity and control over my tongue.

_____ I call my husband's accountability group members to tell on him.

When we regularly submit our marriages to the influence of God's Word, we allow the Holy Spirit to do His work in strengthening and balancing our relationships. Our goal in marriage is to draw closer to each other as we draw closer to God. The following diagram shows what a healthy marriage looks like.

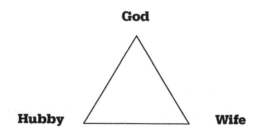

When we choose to live in conflict with God's plans for marriage, we begin to displace the Spirit in the triangle. We actually situate ourselves between our husbands and their connections with the Lord, thus blocking the way of what the Holy Spirit wants to do.

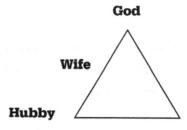

Which triangle best depicts your marriage? Use the blank triangle to illustrate the balance of your relationships with God and your spouse currently.

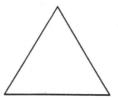

ACTION STEP:
Read Ephesians 1:18-20. This passage speaks about the power that can raise the dead. If your marriage feels lifeless, begin praying for the same power mentioned in Ephesians to heal and restore your relationship with your spouse.

No matter how off balance your triangle may appear, God can help you make improvements! If you despair over the state of your marriage, please seek help—even if you have to find it out of town. Seek wise, godly counsel and remember to keep praying the Word over your marriage. Focus on the one person you can change: you. Keep the faith, and remember that God stands with you through the trials. You can always count on His faithfulness. The Lord wants your marriage strong and healthy. Allow Him to tighten the laces connecting you and your spouse, double knotting them so that nothing can pull them loose.

footprints to follow

Whether trudging through snow or walking along a sandy beach, kids everywhere love to try to step in the larger footprints of their parents. If you've watched your children participate in this game over several seasons, you know that the day comes when little feet begin to outsize the imprints made by mom and dad. Although we moms love to see those feet growing physically, we also want our children to grow beyond us in a spiritual sense. We desire that their footprints make a bigger mark on this world than ours do.

While the spiritual growth of her children is an important issue for every Christian mom, we've found that parents in ministry face unique hurdles as they raise their kids. The following are seven action steps that can help moms meet these specific challenges.

Step 1. Be flexible!

Ministry life demands family flexibility. Sometimes people get sick and dad has to go to the hospital instead of sitting down to a family dinner or attending a child's ball game. Unfortunately, unexpected funerals can shorten vacations. Our challenge as mothers married to ministers is to set the tone for how our kids handle ministry-related interruptions to family life.

Describe the last time your household faced a change of plans due to ministry related circumstances.

How did your kids handle the change of plans?

How did you react to the interruption?

If you notice a correlation between your kids' attitudes and your own, you aren't imagining it. Kids follow mom's lead; you set the tone of the home. It's up to you to influence how your sons and daughters see the responsibility of ministry. You can help them understand the important role your husband plays in helping people deal with life's difficulties. Share how others count on him to remind them of God's love when times get hard. And when the phone rings at an inconvenient time to deliver a sad piece of news about a family in your church, stop and pray for the people involved in that crisis. Not only will your kids learn to go to God first when bad things happen, but they'll learn to better accept disappointments when dad has to change plans.

Remember—and teach your children to remember—nothing that comes your way surprises the Lord. Psalm 37:5-6 states, "Commit your way to the Lord; trust in Him, and He will act making your righteousness shine like the dawn" (HCSB). Start each day with prayer and commit that day to Him, asking for His guidance as you make plans. When changes occur, know that God's in control and allow your response or reaction to glorify Him.

Step 2. Be willing to step up.

Sunday proves one of the most difficult days of the week for ministers' wives. All those little details of helping children remember their weekly Bible verses, tracking down a hair ribbon that matches an outfit, finding a Bible, setting aside their tithes, and making sure everyone gets out the door on time are just a few challenges we must tackle. Other families can go to church and enjoy the worship experience together, often even including dad in the process of helping get the kids ready and out the door without fighting. In ministry families, however, Sunday mornings mean dad goes to work; in fact, he may leave early and stay late. Perhaps he'll even drive separately. This can leave ministry wives feeling like single moms.

Thankfully, we can overcome these very real and difficult challenges, but first let's acknowledge that when we don't handle the stress of this job well, signs of rebellion against dad's job and church in general may follow. Our kids might start to make comments about dad's absence and their frustration of not gaining his ear about something important. We must nip Sunday morning negativity in the bud. Instead of growing angry or bitter about our lack of support, we need to willingly do what's necessary and best for our children.

ACTION STEP:
Someti mes planning ahead can alleviate stress. For instance, setting everyone's Sunday clothes out on Saturday night, putting Bibles and offering envelopes beside the door, and encouraging the kids to review memory verses on the way to service can make for an easier morning. Consider your list of responsibilities. What can you do to ease Sunday stress?

List weekly responsibilities you tackle in relation to your kids' involvement at church.

Read Ephesians 4:29. How can you apply the wisdom of this verse to Sunday mornings at your house?

What's the importance of doing so?

Write Philippians 4:19.

God promises that He will meet all our needs—even our Sunday morning needs. If we'll keep that at the forefront of our thoughts, Sunday mornings will grow easier. Instead of focusing on all the aggravations and tensions that come with Sundays, we must learn to focus on the blessings. When we do we'll become more aware of the joy that comes with knowing our kids are growing in their knowledge of God. We'll learn to more thoroughly appreciate the kindhearted senior adult who meets us in the parking lot to help get the kids out of their car seats or the nursery attendant who always greets our child with a welcoming smile.

Scripture tells us to pray about everything, and that means everything. Make a habit of asking God to give you strength to handle the extra responsibilities that come with your husband's job. Step up to the challenge, knowing that while Sunday mornings aren't always easy, God can help us to set good examples for our children even in the midst of them.

Step 3. Deal with expectations realistically.

Ministry kids live under a cloud of high expectations. Like it or not, people watch you and your children, observing everything from the way they dress to the way they wear their hair to whether or not they run in the church's hallway. Such observations lead to comments and suggestions which can come across as judgmental, but it's important to realize that many people are simply interested in your family and honestly care.

Help your kids know the difference between human expectations and the Lord's. It's up to us to equip our kids to discern which expectations will influence their behavior and lives. Obviously, God's expectations should trump those of other people; but sometimes when bombarded with expectations regarding every part of life, we struggle to remember what matters most.

Comparing an expectation to what God's Word says reveals whether or not we should allow it to become a concern. Some of the expectations those in our church families place on our children are straight from the Word of God and apply to all believers; others reflect only personal preferences and years of tradition. No child will act and look perfect all the time. Small children pitch fits in the church lobby no matter who their parents are. Fourth graders tell whoppers to impress their friends and have burping contests regardless of what dad does for a living. Teenagers make dumb decisions, talk back, and roll their eyes even if their mothers and fathers serve in ministry. Your kids are kids, and that's okay.

Reminding yourself of the difference between expectations from God and those from people can help identify whether an issue needs action or dismissal when people point out supposed "faults" in your children.

Mark the following expectations with a G for "from God" or a P for "from people" to show whether each is from God or people.

___ **Ministers' daughters should always wear dresses to church.**

___ **Ministers' kids must attend every event.**

___ **Ministers' children should tell their friends about Jesus.**

___ **Ministers' kids should respect authority.**

___ **Ministers' children should know all the answers in Sunday School.**

___ **Ministers' kids should never sit in the back row.**

___ **Ministers' kids should always be on time.**

___ **Ministers' children must tell the truth.**

___ **Ministers' kids should model perfect behavior.**

___ **Ministers' kids should read their Bibles.**

Ever made your teen get involved in three Bible studies at once to maintain his or her positive image and set a good example? Ever caught yourself making decisions based on what you think other people expect from ministers' kids? Do you bring your kids to church events even when they are too tired or even sick because you worry what others might think? Understand that not all of the unrealistic expectations your children face come from non-family members. We as moms sometimes commit the same offense. We must learn to make parenting decisions not based on what we think others expect but on what God desires.

Step 4. Guard against a skewed view of God.

Some ministry kids wonder, If serving God is so great, why does it stress my parents out so bad? We've got to realize that because our kids are raised in the ministry, they naturally develop a more realistic view of what ministry is all about. Unfortunately, this closeness to what's going on behind the scenes can lead them to a skewed view of the God we serve as well as a negative view toward the church.

Which of the following do you think best explains your kids' view of God?

- ◯ God doesn't have time for me.
- ◯ God is big and can do anything.
- ◯ I'm scared of God.
- ◯ God is my friend.
- ◯ If God made my family this way, I don't want any part of Him.

Which of the following do you think best explains your kids' views on church in general?

- ◯ Church is a place where I get in trouble.
- ◯ Church is full of hypocrites.
- ◯ I want to serve at a church myself.
- ◯ When I get bigger, I'm gonna do church differently.
- ◯ Church is my favorite place to go.

While many ministry parents may rear children who'll enter ministry themselves, others inadvertently turn their kids away. They may grow so strict and legalistic about the "rules of ministry" that their children want nothing to do with God. They may allow bitterness over very difficult aspects of ministry to drive their kids away from church. Each of us must allow God to rule as head over our homes and actions. The truth is that when your husband's job and your family's role in the church are about God, your kids' perceptions of God and the church are directly impacted. We must do all we can to insure that the ministry's impact on our families is positive.

How can you change your actions to help your children see the positives of ministry?

MISSTEP:

Serving and loving the members of your church is important, but serving and loving your kids is more so. Do you save your best for everyone else and give your kids the leftovers? What can you do for your family to show them they top your list of important people? (Example: Cook a special dinner or treat for your family instead of always saving the best for the church potluck.)

God is faithful, and we must trust Him to do the work He ordains in our kids' lives. As you pray for your kids, don't forget to ask that you make a positive impact on their spiritual lives. Deuteronomy 6:4-9 reminds us to teach spiritual things to our children as we go about our days. Our daily attitude and conversation should reflect and model God's character.

Step 5. Acknowledge peer relationship struggles.

Every ministry kid faces social tensions unique to the territory that become more obvious as they grow older. For instance, staff kids sometimes feel more possessive of and scuffle over dolls and toys in the nursery since they see those toys more often. Middle school kids find themselves taking dares and doing out-of-character things just to assure peers that they are as normal as the next kid. No matter their ages, kids who grow up in ministry notice differences in the way their peers relate to them.

For instance, some guys simply won't date girls whose fathers serve as pastors because they rationalize the girl as off limits. Likewise, some girls will always consider ministers' sons as younger versions of their fathers, as if they are destined to follow the same path as their dads. Even party throwers will sometimes leave out ministers' kids because they fear the pastor will question his children for sordid details of the party that he can preach against. Although from a parent's perspective, such scenarios seem complimentary to guys and girls committed to living for Christ, we must realize that our kids might struggle with feeling left out or excluded.

What struggles do your kid(s) face as a result of your family's ministry?

Paul encourages believers "to walk worthy of the calling you have received" (Ephesians 4:1, HCSB). Ministry kids find that the struggles they face as a result of being set apart as the pastor's children are samples of what they'll face as adults living for Christ. When others make fun or leave them out, they should take it as a compliment and a testimony to the fact that they as Christ-followers live differently. Help them see the big picture of how godly decisions made now will help them make healthy choices that will define the rest of their lives. Remind them of the wisdom of 1 Peter 2:11-12: "Dear friends, I urge you ... Conduct yourselves honorably ... so that in a case where they speak against you as those who do evil, they may, by observing your good works, glorify God" (HCSB).

We should repeatedly assure our kids that the opinions of others do not define them. They are God's children, and His opinion matters most. The frustrations they face are often a direct result of the fact that people fear letting the light of those who live for Christ get too close to what's really going on in their lives; light may reveal things they don't

want to confront. Moms can help kids see the positives of how endur-
ing trials for the faith now builds a foundation that won't give way as
life's issues grow.

**How can you encourage your children
through tough situations with their peers?
(For example: Ease the pain of being left
out of the big event by planning a fun alter-
native option and allow your kids to bring
some friends.)**

Before we move from our discussion on peer struggles, we need to
mention the fact that some people want to befriend your kids only
because they are staff kids. When people pump our kids for details on
our families or use them as pawns to grow closer to the minister, children feel used or manipulated.

Protect your kids from unhealthy relationships as best you can,
and stay sensitive to hurt feelings that can come from these situations.
Keep them covered in prayer and remember that sometimes missing
a youth social to spend some time alone with God can make a huge
difference. Be careful not to let avoiding their troubles become a habit.

Step 6. Handle unsolicited advice carefully.

Sometimes it seems since the church hires ministry families, every
member feels free to share their thoughts and advice on how we should
raise our children. We've heard words of wisdom on every subject from
dressing our kids, covering babies' heads, getting rid of pacifiers, how
to get pregnant, breastfeeding, teenage piercing, talking back, healthy
eating habits for picky kids, and sleep issues. "Your teenager was driv-

ing too fast in the church parking lot. ... You need to teach your child to share; he bit someone in the nursery. ... When is your son getting a haircut? His hair is too long. ... You need to pick out your daughter's clothing yourself; her taste is too wild. ... You have to get your kid potty trained; it's too much work to keep the nursery now. ... Your kids are running through the halls and jumping on the stage after the service; you need to teach them to be still and reverent." The advice seems endless. The real question is, how should we handle it?

Which of the following best describes your typical response to unsolicited advice?

- ○ **I bristle and say, "Mind your own business!"**
- ○ **I stress out and determine to apply the advice.**
- ○ **I prayerfully consider the advice and apply it if I think it's sound.**
- ○ **I ignore it and make a mental note to avoid the advice-giver.**

FUN FLIPS:

What's the funniest advice a church member has given you? The best or most helpful?

God can give us discernment to discover what advice we need to apply and what we should toss. When we approach advice and comments positively, we may get some good out of them. We find that when we prayerfully consider advice and thank people for their concern for our families we sometimes discover several nuggets of useful wisdom and even random tidbits to file away for the future.

Sometimes advice comes at the point when you feel particularly vulnerable about a subject. Understand that when we can be real, admit our failures, not stress out over motherhood (who is perfect anyway?), and learn to laugh at ourselves, we'll discover that people don't mean to condemn us for our shortcomings; they simply care enough to get involved.

Try not to hear all advice as implied criticism. Ask yourself, "Am I doing something with my kids that invites comments and criticism because it's so outside the norm?" If you find that your answer is "yes" but the differences spring from a godly conviction, then celebrate that people notice a difference between your kids and others. If your answer is "yes," but the differences reflect only your preferences or style, evaluate whether or not you need to make changes.

Above all, remember that God has entrusted your precious children to you and your husband and you are accountable to Him for the choices you make. People may offer excellent suggestions or help, but not all the advice you receive is worthy of consideration. If you honestly feel it stems from wrong motives, maliciousness, or even ignorance—don't take it to heart.

Step 7. Teach them to appreciate the perks.

Ministry families receive many added blessings and special gifts that other families don't. Involve your kids in celebrating the positives of living in a ministry home. Point out all the good things that come to your family because of dad's job: things like free tickets to a ballgame, fresh homemade bread, and baskets of homegrown produce. Help them develop an attitude of appreciation.

Over time, some ministry families begin to develop a sense of entitlement or expectation that certain things are due them because they serve. We need to be sure that our children appreciate the good things or perks that come their way because of ministry, but that they don't begin to expect them. Remember, when your husband's sixth anniversary goes unannounced after a churchwide celebration on his fifth, not to get bitter and complain. Instead, reflect on all those times when someone took your kids to the pizza place, helped you repaint your kitchen, fixed you dinner, or sent a card. It's those little things that remind us of the differences we as ministry families make in peoples' lives. Help your children to see them in that light, too.

How do people show their appreciation for your family?

Raising kids and juggling ministry can be tough at times, but God will supply all the answers for our parenting struggles if only we'll ask. None of us are alone; He gave us a family of believers who can help. Many joys come with raising children, but we wholeheartedly agree with the apostle John: "I have no greater joy than to hear that my children are walking in the truth." (3 John 4). May our footsteps continually lead them toward godliness.

Before we close, we'd like to share a few tips from some kids well acquainted with ministry life:

"If you've got to tell a story about me for an illustration, please ask first."

"Please don't discipline with the line, 'because you're the pastor's kid.' That makes me crazy."

"Don't make me feel like I've always got to have the right answer at church."

"Help me know I'm not less important than your next group study."

"Be consistent with what you preach and teach at church when you're home with me."

"Be authentic and real with me."

"Please let me be a regular kid instead of making me feel like I have to be perfect."

"Don't be strict. Let me eat ice cream for supper sometimes."

ACTION STEP: Many perks and blessings accompany raising kids while serving in ministry. List a few and challenge your family to add to the list.

"Please talk to the people who get onto me more than they do the other kids at church. Tell them I'm just a kid, too."

"Act like you are still my mom at church. Don't make me feel like just an interruption."

peace lovin' combat boots

FUN FLIPS:

How would you title
a chapter on spiritual
warfare? What graphic
would you choose
to support the idea?
Explain

Recently we engaged in our favorite form of exercise torture: a spin class. As we groaned and sweated, struggling to keep pace on our stationary bicycles, the instructor said, "Come on girls, find your comfort zone and ride!" We exchanged glances and laughed out loud at the thought of finding any comfort in a class as painful as spinning. The idea seemed a ridiculous oxymoron, definitely contradicting itself.

The Christian life challenges believers to embrace a seemingly crazy notion—we should live at peace while also waging spiritual war. Since that's the case, lace up those peace lovin' combat boots as we address this difficult issue.

The Bible supports the notion that spiritual warfare requires us to approach life with both preparation (signified by the boots) and an application of the peace that comes with knowing that God controls all things. Ephesians 6:12 warns believers, "For our battle is not against flesh and blood, but against the rulers, against the authorities, against the world powers of this darkness, against the spiritual forces of evil in the heavens" (HCSB). This indicates that Christ-followers live in the spiritual trenches, daily waging a righteous war against the enemy's schemes. Spiritual warfare intensifies for those of us who serve in ministry; that's why we must stay armed and ready to meet it head-on.

Why do you think ministry families might find themselves more susceptible to spiritual warfare than those who aren't serving?

Describe a situation in which you feel your family experienced spiritual warfare.

The Bible says all believers will face spiritual battles against a very real enemy (see 1 Peter 5:8-9), but those who commit to ministry move to the front lines of the battlefield. We believe that serving in active, daily ministry leaves us more open to warfare for three main reasons.

Reason 1: Our life goal contradicts Satan's plans.

The devil's primary objective? Keep lost people lost. One of his favorite tactics in accomplishing this is to keep saved people feeling discouraged and useless. As we desire to see people come to know the Lord and strive to help believers to grow and mature spiritually, Satan does everything possible to make our efforts ineffective. He will use any available scheme to distract us from our purpose.

Reason 2: Our sphere of influence makes us strategic targets.

Because of our positions of leadership in ministry, people look to us and our husbands for spiritual guidance. This means that if Satan can cause us to stumble, he can twist our failings into a hurdle affecting far more people than just us. Scripture challenges us to live above reproach (1 Timothy 3:2) and even mentions that getting tossed into a lake with a millstone around your neck is preferable to leading other people astray (Luke 17:2). Since we as Christians represent God as ambassadors here on earth, what we do and say either reinforces the truth about Him or gives people a false impression. That old adage "You may be the only Jesus someone sees" points to a reality that makes the devil take aim in our direction.

The way we choose to live has a huge impact on those around us. Write your name in the circle. Then label each long line with the names of places where you interact with others.

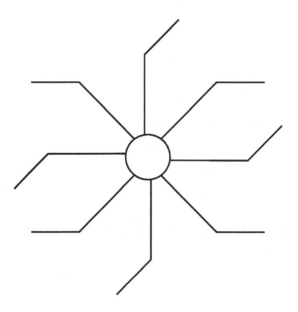

On the smaller lines, write the names of people at each place with whom you interact. Draw more lines as needed.

What do you need to do differently to better point people to Christ?

Reason 3: Our behind-the-scenes knowledge can test the strength of our armor.

The final reason that we as ministry wives face a heavy barrage of enemy fire comes down to the fact that we can appear easy targets. Who better to discourage in her walk with the Lord than the pastor's wife who's heard so many unpleasant details about ministry and church issues that she teeters on the edge of burnout? We must realize that allowing our in-depth knowledge of certain situations to lead into ungodly thinking presents a danger. It can leave cracks in our spiritual armor in the form of a sinful attitude or unforgiving spirit—both easy targets for an enemy bent on destruction.

Which of the following statements could set you up as an "easy target" for the enemy? Check all that apply.

- ○ **"If the church knew the details of what that leader did, they wouldn't be so nice to him."**
- ○ **"He made a mistake. God forgave him. I do too."**
- ○ **"She better not pretend like everything is ok. I know what she said."**
- ○ **"I would never be so gullible as to ..."**
- ○ **"I'll never be able to look her in the eye again after all that happened."**

Each of these statements, with the exception of the second one, could serve as a foothold for the devil. We've got to remain on guard against negative attitudes and complaints.

The Christian life isn't easy, especially for those who serve in ministry. Spiritual warfare is not a result of failings in your walk with the Lord. In fact, if you aren't experiencing any spiritual warfare, you either aren't really saved, don't recognize it as it happens, or you live as a non-threatening Christian. Satan generally chooses to focus his energy against those who make a difference in this lost world.

Don't read that last sentence as an excuse for checking out spiritually and becoming a non-threatening believer. Though we as ministry wives face a heightened threat of attack, we are neither defenseless nor alone. The Lord will use our commitment to stand for Him to deepen our relationships with Him and to guide others to His side; the victories are worth the fight!

The key to this issue is not to learn how to avoid spiritual warfare but to learn to recognize it when it comes. In doing so, we gain a sense of urgency in our preparations and determination to resist the enemy.

Understand that we aren't suggesting that you start to look for little demons behind every bush, but we do encourage you to remain on the lookout for the devil's advances so that you can better prepare to handle them God's way.

Put a checkmark beside each of the following scenarios that might point to a case of spiritual warfare.

○ **Your husband begins teaching a series on marriage, and your own begins to suffer.**

○ **Shame over past choices leads you to stop reading your Bible.**

○ **Church starts in ten minutes and you can't find one of your high heels.**

○ **Your phone keeps ringing through the hour you've set aside for prayer.**

○ **You find yourself attracted to a nice man at work.**

○ **On the way home from a revival meeting, your tire goes flat.**

○ **Numerous distractions interrupt an Easter service as the gospel is shared.**

○ **Your child's grades suffer as a one-week revival stretches into three.**

○ **Right before a big sermon series starts, the climate in your home shifts and no one gets along.**

○ **Feelings of inferiority, uselessness, and hopelessness discourage you from staying active in church.**

Although we hesitate to label any situation "warfare," true warfare does differ from the average bad day or tough circumstance. For instance, when you let your children stay up extra late on Saturday night and they have a hard time getting to church on time the next day; you experience a consequence, not a spiritual battle. Furthermore, claiming "the devil made me do it" after choosing to live in the flesh and make bad decisions is a cop out, not proof of Satan's attack. A good rule of thumb in identifying what spiritual warfare is not is to ask ourselves, "Did my sin or poor choice lead me to face this consequence?" If the answer is "yes," we may be surrendering to our flesh nature, effectively accomplishing the devil's work for him. Sometimes our greatest enemy is ourselves.

Describe a time when you blamed Satan for your own bad choices. How did doing so impact your walk with the Lord?

Your relationship with others?

MISSTEP: Hanging on to bad habits and the tendency to make poor choices prevents us from making positive changes that align us with God. What habits do you need to relinquish in order to walk more closely with the Lord? What can you do to make better choices?

Read Romans 14:12. Why can't we excuse or overlook our sins?

In 1 Peter 2:11, the apostle says, "Dear friends, I urge
you, as aliens and strangers in the world, to abstain
from sinful desires, which war against your soul." How
might unconfessed sin make us more susceptible to
spiritual warfare? Check all that apply.

○ It tarnishes our witness.
○ It suggests we're no threat to the enemy.
○ It waves a sign over our heads that says, "Pick
on me! I'm down."
○ It makes us feel defeated.
○ It has no impact.

Although sin continually threatens to hinder our relationships with
Christ, we don't have to let our weaknesses and failures ruin our effectiveness. The good news is that when we confess our sins He is faithful
to forgive us and cleanse us (1 John 1:9). Romans 8:37,39 assures us
that "we are more than conquerors through [Christ] who love[s] us ...
nothing shall be able to separate us from the love of God" (NKJV). So
if the struggles you face are not warfare, deal with them according to
Scripture and move on in victory.

You probably notice that things tend to get crazy around major
spiritual highs such as the week of a great revival or just before an
awesome youth camp. Likely your husband experiences his own
"Holy Hangovers" after each sermon or teaching time, and you may
find yourself struggling with the spiritual blahs from time-to-time. In
those seasons when spiritual warfare comes your way, your standard
operating procedure could include anything from hiding under the
covers in denial, getting mad and fighting back, retreating out of fear,
or even persevering till the end. But it's important to realize that every
response will either help or exacerbate a situation. How you deal with
warfare can either diffuse the enemy or intensify the battle.

**How did Elijah react to the threat posed by Jezebel?
(see 1 Kings 18-19)**

Elijah, empowered by God, spoke boldly in front of all the prophets of
Baal. He called fire from heaven to burn up the altar and prove God's
identity and ability. Yet in the face of this huge spiritual and national
victory, Elijah hit a low. He went from bold and victorious to scared,
fearful, and hopeless. His roller coaster ride of emotions reflects a
tendency common to those in ministry.

**Do you think Elijah's actions in the face of threats from
an enemy, helped his situation or made things worse?
Explain.**

**How did Job respond to the attack on his family and
livelihood in Job 1:6-22?**

Job, a man who loved God, found himself under attack because of his
righteousness. Though he experienced great personal loss and pain,
Job remained convinced that God was in charge and in the right. His
determination to stay loyal to God when the road grew rough makes him
an excellent example for Christians who find themselves in warfare.

What does Job's story teach us about the role of attitude during times of warfare?

Read Luke 4:1-13. What affect did Christ's words have on Satan's attack? What's the significance of this to our discussion on spiritual warfare?

ACTION STEP:
Write Ephesians 6:10-18 on a card and carry it with you. The next time you find yourself in the direct line of fire from the enemy, post the card where you see it throughout the day and determine to stand firm.

Elijah's retreat and regroup response to spiritual warfare reflects the way many of us deal with the subject. We panic when it comes and complain when things don't go smoothly. Job's humble attitude of acceptance, on the other hand, reflects an attitude that we should adopt as we choose to trust God in the midst of struggle. Christ responded to warfare by remaining focused on the Father and by applying Scripture to every temptation—His approach demonstrates a habit we must emulate.

Ephesians 6:10-18 is one of the most powerful passages dealing with spiritual warfare. As you read, notice the underlined words. Each is a directional command that calls for action.

Finally, be strengthened by the Lord and by His vast strength. Put on the full armor of God so that you can stand against the tactics of the Devil. For our battle is not against flesh and blood, but against the rulers, against the authorities, against the world powers of this darkness, against the spiritual forces of evil in the heavens. This is why you must take up the full armor of God, so that you may be able to resist in the evil day, and having prepared

everything, to take your stand. Stand, therefore, with truth
like a belt around your waist, righteousness like armor on
your chest, and your feet sandaled with readiness for the
gospel of peace. In every situation take the shield of faith,
and with it you will be able to extinguish the flaming
arrows of the evil one. Take the helmet of salvation, and
the sword of the Spirit, which is God's word. With every
prayer and request, pray at all times in the Spirit, and stay
alert in this, with all perseverance and intercession for all
the saints. (HCSB)

Paul's advice to believers is clear: you must intentionally put on spiritual armor to protect yourself from the enemy's attacks. Each of us
should take time to regularly evaluate our spiritual readiness for battle.
Are you secure in your salvation? Do you choose to live in righteousness? Do your choices reflect the truth of God's Word? What about your
shield of faith, do people see it and know to whom you belong? Is peace
a part of your life? Are you prayed up and alert? If so, then stand firm.

Label the arrows with ways in which you feel attacked.
(i.e., discouragement, marital problems)

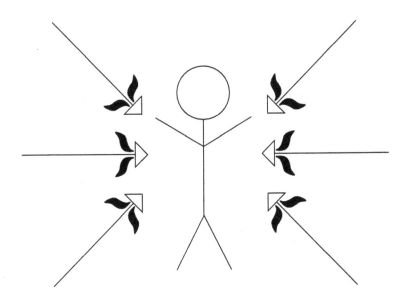

What effect, according to Ephesians 6:16, does arming ourselves with righteousness, faith, and peace have on the arrows the enemy sends our way?

Make no mistake; the devil's "fiery darts" will come, but our shield will extinguish those arrows (see Ephesians 6:16). The battles may grow intense and cause very real pain and hurt. However, we can find comfort in the fact that armed readiness protects us from his advances as well as assuring us that God is on His throne. We will win in the end.

In many experiences with major situations of warfare, you may find that time stands still and the situation demands complete focus. Sometimes we get so bogged down in stress and anxiety that it's challenging not to let the pain or fear paralyze us. In such times, we should remember that men and women of the Bible faced similar tendencies. Moses, for instance, feared speaking to Pharaoh in part because of his insecurities; but he stood firm in the face of the Egyptian army and literally stepped out into uncharted waters. Though he was undeniably afraid, he chose to obediently trust God even when it looked like the bad guys held the advantage. His decision to stay focused on the Lord neutralized the enemy's ability to discourage him.

In what situations did/do you allow fear to keep you from following God in obedience?

What can you do to limit or neutralize the enemy's influence?

If fear of warfare or anxiety over the problems associated with building a new church building, leading a small group, or reaching out to a neighbor hold you back from following God's plans, don't give up. You can do whatever God calls you to do.

The Bible says that with God all things are possible (Matthew 19:26): you can survive spiritual warfare and even grow through it. The next time the enemy sends those flaming arrows your way, know that Satan wouldn't bother you unless you're up to something he doesn't like. Keep your armor ready and lace up those peace-lovin' combat boots; the Lord will use you to advance His kingdom!

Dear Minister's Wife:

On behalf of LifeWay, thank you for your service supporting your minister husband and your church. We appreciate the huge load you both carry. We've heard from many wives that church leadership, while rewarding, is often frustrating and even discouraging. We see ministry families leaving the ministry daily due to the stresses they encounter.

The enemy wants to make sure that you and your husband lose focus, get disillusioned in ministry, and even doubt your calling. But God is more powerful than the enemy and has a great plan to use you to touch lives through your faithful journey with Him.

Ministers' wives struggle at times to build safe relationships. LifeWay's goal to help churches includes helping individuals experience spiritual transformation. We pray this study will help you become comfortable in your very special "shoes" and then to encourage one another as you walk together.

Thank you for taking the time to delve into the Word as you grow as a ministry wife. Our churches need you and rely on you. Thank you again for your faithfulness to obey God's call in your life, first as a woman, as a wife, some as a mother, then as a ministry supporter. As you model godliness in your life, in both joys and struggles, those around you will be encouraged to trust God in their circumstances. Please visit our web site www.lifeway.com/women.

With much love and appreciation,

Chris Adams
Senior Lead Women's Ministry Specialist
LifeWay Christian Resources

sole sisters

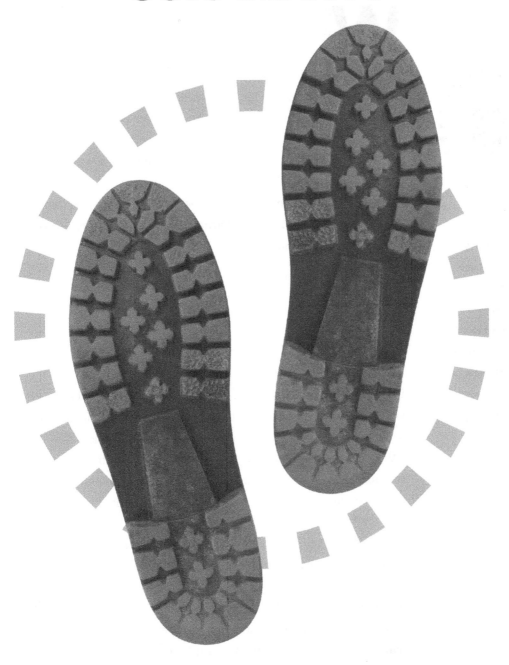

What do tea rooms, pedicures, and shopping share? All are better when experienced with a friend. Dining at frou-frou places with scented candles and lace tablecloths, having our nails done, and hitting a great sale are just more fun with some girlfriends at your side. That's because God created us with a need for fellowship which is better met when we spend time with some "sole" sisters—women who connect with you on a deeper level, accept you the way you are, and love you enough to want God's best for you.

List the names of friends whom you count as "sole" sisters. Beside each name, list things that make those friendships special.

FUN FLIP:

List your favorite things to do with your girlfriends. Pick one and plan to do it soon. Consider someone new you might need to reach out to or choose to meet with some old friends. Either way, enjoy a great time!

Different schools of thoughts circulate regarding whether or not the wives of ministers should develop friendships within the church. Some say, "Ministers' wives, keep your friendships outside the church." Others insist, "It's your job to be best friends with all the deacons' wives." Still others say, "You can't make friends with only a few women in the congregation. You need to get close with them all."

While we've heard all these comments covering the extremes, we think—in light of our own experiences—that it's important to develop a healthy view of friends in general before deciding what approach works best for you at your particular church. Friends play a vital role in our lives. That's why we need to learn how to treat friendships according to the guidelines in Scripture. When we do, we can gain discernment on both choosing friends and relating to them in a godly fashion.

Look up the following verses and list each characteristic of friendship you find under either the positive or negative heading.

	POSITIVE	NEGATIVE
Proverbs 11:13	trustworthy	gossip
Proverbs 17:9		
Proverbs 17:17		
Proverbs 18:24		
Proverbs 22:24		
Proverbs 25:19		
2 Timothy 4:16-17		
Ecclesiastes 4:9-10		

Review the character traits we should look for in potential friends. Describe your best long-time friend.

How does your relationship with her compare with biblical friendship? List the positives and negatives.

ACTION STEP:
Write a note to friends who either invested in you early on or who currently spend time with you. Thank them for their impact on you.

You may serve in a church where people seek you out and want to be your friend because you're a staff wife, or you may work in a church where it seems no one wants your friendship for the same reason. Let's face it: friendships present complicated issues for most people in ministry. We know God created us for fellowship with other people, but we aren't always sure with whom to form those close relationships.

Complete the following statement: I typically form friendships with ...

○ other staff wives.
○ church members.
○ neighbors.
○ people outside our church family.
○ my kids' friends' moms.
○ people who live out of town.
○ no one. I don't have friends.

No matter how you answered that last question, realize that the Lord does not want you friendless or isolated. Even if you don't currently have someone to whom you can pour out all your thoughts and feelings, God's Word says that we can and should "pour out [our] hearts to God for He is [our] refuge" (Psalm 62:8). The Lord directs us to call on Him first when life gets overwhelming, but He recognizes our natural tendency to share feelings with others and offers many Scriptures on how to choose friends wisely.

Complete the following sentence: When something big happens, I speed dial ...

○ my husband.
○ a friend.
○ a mentor.
○ Mom.
○ God.

Jesus taught us by example not to expect from others what only God can do. In the garden, Christ's friends couldn't stay awake with Him in His greatest hour of need, but God stayed at His side. Your friends are human, they will let you down, just as the disciples let Jesus down. Though Jesus counted His followers as friends, He didn't need them in order to feel complete.

Like Jesus, we too must cultivate a healthy outlook on friend-ships so that we don't place a burden on our friends that they can't bear. When we begin to rely on a person instead of Jesus, our lives become dangerously unbalanced.

Look at the illustration and prayerfully consider which side of the scale you typically assign to Jesus. Write His name on that side. On the other side, list the names of those people on whom you also rely.

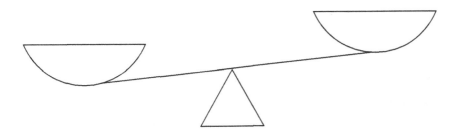

Giving more weight to our relationship with Christ than we do to our friendships actually serves to protect us. While God will never let us down, friends sometimes will. We find it interesting that although Jesus knew Judas would ultimately betray Him, He still included him among the Twelve. (Matthew 26:21)

This doesn't mean that we should seek out people who will betray us, but it does encourage us to take the chance on developing godly friendships even though they come with no guarantee. When and if betrayal comes, we have the love and support of Jesus. He knows how much it hurts when people let us down, after all, He's been there.

Briefly describe an experience in which you felt betrayed by a friend.

Did you see any signs warning of an unhealthy relationship prior to this situation?

What did you learn from the experience?

Many who serve on church staffs fear letting others get too close because they've fallen victim to betrayal in the form of revealed confidences and broken trust. Perhaps a friend with whom you opened your heart blabbed what you shared to ten others. Maybe a married couple you and your husband used to go out to dinner with secretly engaged in affairs. Maybe a fellow staff person and long-time friend got caught in embezzlement. In any case, when those close to us let us down, it's easy to go into retreat and hide mode. We've got to remember that when we close ourselves off from forming new friendships, we leave ourselves open to loneliness that often leads to other issues.

Isolation left untreated can lead directly to a state of depression. None of us are immune to it. If you struggle with this tendency, know that depression is neither an unpardonable sin nor an untreatable illness. In their book, *Rediscovering Church*, Bill and Lynne Hybels shared Lynne's honest description of how she dealt with loneliness, depression, and isolation as a young minister's wife. If the pastor's wife at a megachurch, surrounded by a large staff, could feel isolated and lonely then it's a reminder that any of us could. That's why we must learn to protect ourselves from isolation. The first step is recognizing factors in our lives that leave us vulnerable to it.

Read through the following list of isolation factors, placing a star beside any that apply to your own situation.

A cold church climate: Sometimes a church's demographics or rigid schedules leave little time for friendship building. If you are the only person your age in attendance and the parking lot empties quickly on Sunday mornings, you may struggle with loneliness.

Stage of life factors: If you are caught up with having babies, home-schooling, or shuttling yours kids to soccer practice, you may find it difficult to make friends.

Unfamiliar surroundings: If you don't know your way around the community or if your church reaches out to a large region, building friendships seems intimidating.

A wall of negative past experiences: If you've built walls around your life for your own protection because of past betrayals, you may not feel free to be yourself. Warming up to new relationships may present a challenge.

> **A precedent of isolation: Sometimes the ministers' wives who go before us establish a tradition of isolation. Changing these precedents can take time.**
>
> **Personal insecurity: If personal insecurities keep you from reaching out to others, you may find yourself wanting to avoid relationships altogether.**
>
> **A fear of moving: If you resist getting close to others because you know God may call you to leave them, you might find yourself encouraging potential friends to turn away.**

No matter which isolation factors hold the greatest pull in your life, don't grow discouraged and don't give up! Proverbs 18:1 says, "One who isolates himself pursues [selfish] desires; he rebels against all sound judgment." That means that remaining cut off from the company of others is a choice; we can do something about it. Isolation is for contagious diseases, not Christians.

As we consider this topic, we're reminded of our own struggles with loneliness and the solutions we've discovered. Breaking from the style to this point, we each want to share a story.

Jennifer's story: I remember when David took his first position as pastor of a small church. I waited about a year for someone to reach out to me and become a friend I could count on. I thought maybe another, more experienced pastor's wife in the area would mentor me or at the least just encourage me. That didn't happen.

I finally realized that younger wives moving to the area might benefit from my outreach and encouragement. I went to the denominational association director in our area and asked if we could start a get-together for ministers' wives at least once a quarter. He agreed, and I began to contact wives and invite them to our first gathering. We weren't a large group and we only met once a quarter, but I gained so much encouragement from meeting with those women! In fact, I now count one of them among my best friends.

Rachel's story: When Jeff and I served at a larger church that had many staff wives, I quickly recognized that I was both the youngest and the newest. That left me feeling disconnected and lonely. One day I looked around and realized that lots of other women around me had small kids and babies the same ages as my own. Instead of sitting at home waiting for a friend to drop in my lap, I decided to invite over a few women with similar aged kids. We had such a great time that we began a weekly ritual of play groups that moved from house to house. We moms found fellowship (which we needed) and the kids got to play with different friends (which they needed).

If you can relate to either of our stories or found your own situation reflected in any of the isolation factors, acknowledge the issue you're up against and determine to overcome it. If you feel lonely and isolated, know that someone may be waiting for you to take the initiative. Someone may need you to step in and befriend her.

What has helped you break through isolation barriers and find friends?

In the columns below, explain how you can proactively and positively deal with isolation issues you now face.

What I'm Facing   **What I can do about it**

MISSTEP:

Some isolation situations result from grudges held or hurt feelings. If you've pulled away from someone because of a personal hurt, what can you do to mend the relationship or move past it to a new one?

When life grows tough because of personal struggles with aging parents and busy children, even the most devoted friends among us may find ourselves letting our relationships with others take a back seat. In fact, it's normal to want to retreat and stay away from people when our lives begin demanding more energy and work than we can give. While some situations may require you to take a break from involved friendships, don't forget that the Lord gives us friendships and expects us to invest in them. We need a game plan for getting back to healthy relationships.

One very important, simple act can solidify and strengthen your friendships. Proverbs 18:24 states, "A man who has friends must himself be friendly" (NKJV). Whether you need to reestablish contact with a friend or are seeking new ones, you must reach out in kindness.

List some practical ways you can put Proverbs 18:24 into practice.

    1.

    2.

    3.

On the scale, rate yourself as a friend.

1	10

Who needs friends anyway?   You can count on me!

What do you need to do differently to become a better friend?

ACTION STEP:

List your weaknesses and strengths as a friend. Write an action plan to improve on your weaknesses then put it into practice.

Self-evaluation provides a fairly clear indicator of how well we support our friends. Routinely evaluating how well our friends support us, however, is equally important to friendship maintenance. True sole sisters don't just take; they help replenish and refresh one another, while challenging each other spiritually. Scripture describes this as "iron sharpening iron" (Proverbs 27:17).

Think of one of your friendships. How well do you support each other?

- ○ **Perfectly. We give and take.**
- ○ **Well, if I'm honest, I think I take more than I contribute.**
- ○ **Not at all. I do all the giving and she does all the taking. I feel used.**
- ○ **I think our friendship feels dry on both sides.**

We need to explore two additional key elements in godly relationships—the biblical concepts of mentoring and discipleship. We need people who invest in us just as much as we are called to invest in others.

Draw a stick figure representing you with a horizontal line pointing to your head. Identify those who currently invest in you and write their names on the line.

Draw lines coming out from your hands. Write on these the names of those in whom you spiritually invest (i.e., your children, the students you teach).

Congratulations, your picture illustrates both accountability and discipleship. These disciplines are both intentional and purposeful. Just as you chose to draw the figure—under duress or willingly— you choose to include these in your life. If this activity proved difficult for you, begin praying that God will bring someone into your life to mentor you and others whom you can disciple.

Remember, good friendships build accountability. The term accountability means "subject to having to report, explain, or justify." If you wonder about the importance accountability plays in a believer's life, turn on your television or read your newspaper. What does the media say about Christ followers? Little reporting surrounds the Christians who do life biblically, but if one prominent believer slips, the media swarms over the story. None of us make good, godly decisions all the time on our own. That's why we need people to give wise counsel no matter how painful it might seem at the moment (see Proverbs 11:14).

When shopping for a new pair of jeans, you might need the help of a wise friend who will tell you if the pair you love actually emphasizes something you don't want to emphasize. You know what we mean. While her honesty may hurt at first, it will help you avoid embarrassment and may even lead to a better choice. This same concept applies to spiritual accountability. We need friends who speak the truth in love and ask us the tough questions like "Did you have your quiet time?", "How's your thought life?", or "Did your words and actions toward your family glorify God today?"

To whom are you accountable?

Did you list the Lord? What about your husband? We are all accountable to God as our Creator. (Genesis 1:27) and to our husbands who love us. In a godly marriage, both parties should remain accountable to the other for things such as how time, money, and energy are spent. Lack of communication and trust over basic issues only leads to problems.

A word of caution. Even if you share the greatest relationship in the world with your spouse, you may not want him as your only source of accountability. As a woman, you need female friends who can hold you accountable in things and situations your spouse may not understand or even be interested in.

Which of the following topics do you feel most comfortable discussing with another woman?

Potty training   Breastfeeding

hormonal issues   discipline   exercise routines

eating habits   thought life   finances

entertainment choices   clothes

bargain shopping   hairstyles   Bible Study

Scripture memorization   wrinkle cream   cellulite treatments

Whatever the issues you choose to discuss with your girlfriends, remember that accountability relationships require not just that we ask the tough questions but that we listen with non-judgmental ears. The different aspects of our relationships will manifest themselves in various ways according to our personalities, lifestyles, stages of life, and spiritual needs. In every case, we must remember that true sole sisters remain intentional about accountability. Whether at the coffee shop, on a play date, or on a girls' night out, we as Christian friends share the responsibility of helping one another stay on track with the Lord.

God may give you one friend or group to hold you accountable in many areas, but He'll sometimes provide in different ways such as a friend who holds you accountable to exercise and three friends who do Bible Study with you. In any case, don't be afraid to ask women to "do life" with you. Always be prayerful and careful as you share until a friend proves herself an authentic 'sole sister,' determined to encourage and support you in your walk with the Lord.

If you don't already enjoy accountability relationships like those we've discussed, pray that God will direct you to the person or persons who will meet this need for you. Ask Him to bring you friends who will remain real and honest. Remember, "sole" sisters' are the polish on the pedicure of life: all our toes look cuter with a little decoration!

As we close, please know that while we can't physically sit beside you as you navigate life's challenges, our hearts are with you. We're honored that you chose to take this journey with us and hope you feel blessed by it. Please take what you've learned in this work and let God do His thing in your life. Know that we love and appreciate you. We believe that "He who started a good work in you will carry it on to completion" (Philippians 1:6). One day we'll share our stories as we gather around the throne. Until then, remember that we—and many others—do walk in shoes much like yours!

We would love to hear from you, and if you have time to let us know how God used this study in your life we would appreciate it. Send any comments or questions to us at either our blog:

http://inourshoesthestudy.wordpress.com/ or to

rachel@rachellovingood.com.

Thanks for taking the time dig in the Word with us!

Joyfully,
Rachel and Jennifer

helpful hints

Baby shower invites, wedding invitations, and graduation announcements routinely fill the mailboxes of many ministry families. Sometimes
ministry wives need to entertain at the drop of a hat or sit in on a serious counseling session after a hectic day with the kids. We've found
that the more prepared we are for the planned and unexpected, the
easier it will be to handle whatever comes our way. The following
suggestions and ideas help us to navigate ministry-related challenges.
We hope they'll do the same for you.

Inexpensive Gift Ideas

For the Staff and/or deacons

1. Purchase leftover ornaments the day after Christmas. They
   make nice gifts for next year, if you can find them when that
   time comes.
2. Buy plain, small terra cotta pots and plant a bulb in each one.
   Tie a bow around top.
3. Purchase gift books and inscribe them with a date, occasion,
   and your greeting.
4. Create a batch of ready-to-make hot chocolate or spiced tea
   mix. Place enough for several servings into a bag tied with
   ribbon and set the package inside a pretty mug. Don't forget
   to include preparation suggestions.

HOT COCOA RECIPE

1 eight-quart box of instant powdered milk

1 pound box confectioner's sugar

2 lb. box chocolate drink mix

6 oz. jar of powdered coffee creamer

Mix ingredients together. Allow for three tsp of mix per one cup of water. Makes a lot.

SPICED TEA MIX

1/3 cup instant tea

1 cup sugar

1 7oz. jar of Tang®

1 10oz. can of lemonade mix (unsweetened)

1 tsp. cinnamon

1 tsp. cloves

Combine all ingredients. Allow for two teaspoons of mix per one cup of boiling water. Serves about 15.

5. Fun food gifts. Stock up on inexpensive all-occasion and Christmas plates and bags and fill them with homemade goodies. A little plastic wrap and curly ribbon tie make for attractive presentation. The following recipes make fun foods that go a long way:

WHITE CANDY

1 lb. peanuts

1 lb. cashews

1 lb. pecans

1 bag pretzels

1 can coconut

1 box honey graham crackers

2 lbs. white chocolate

Mix all ingredients but the chocolate. Melt chocolate. Pour over mix. Let cool. Break apart. Makes a huge amount!

CHRISTMAS BARK

Melt 1 pound of white chocolate and break up peppermint candies into it. Put on tray to cool. Break apart and place in Christmas tins or in cellophane paper with tie around top.

TING-A-LINGS

1 bag of chocolate chips
1 bag butterscotch chips
1 bag of chow mein noodles
1 can of peanuts

Melt chips together and then add noodles and peanuts. Mix together and drop by spoonfuls on waxed paper.

CROCK-POT™ CANDY

In a cold Crock-Pot, layer the following ingredients* in this order:

1 can salted peanuts
1 can unsalted peanuts (or use salted again)
1 bar German chocolate broken up
½ bag peanut butter chips
1 bag chocolate chips (either milk or semisweet)
½ bag white chocolate chips

*Substitutions are fine. Turn Crock-Pot on low heat for 2 hours. Stir and drop by spoonfuls onto wax paper.

For Baby Showers

1. Purchase generic or neutral-colored sleepers or blankets on clearance so you can use them for girls or boys. Stock up on blue or pink rattles or smaller items to put with the neutral item.
2. Buy books on memory making, child rearing, devotions for families, or even children's Bible storybooks that helped you raise your children. Many titles are available online for a fraction of their in-store price.
3. Buy attractive baby picture frames at discount stores and use them to frame gift cards for local photographers.

For Bridal Showers

1. Stock up on attractive kitchen utensils and hand towels. Three or four wooden utensils or spoons tied with a dish towel for a bow make a nice gift.
2. Buy a stash of Emilie Barnes' books on home management. You may get a better price if you buy in bulk.
3. Fill a laundry basket with cleaning supplies.
4. Buy a Springform® pan or loaf pan and tie an easy, favorite recipe to it. For instance:

> **OREO® CAKE RECIPE**
> **Top layer:**
> **1 small instant chocolate pudding**
> **1 small instant vanilla pudding**
> **3 cups milk**

Middle layer:

1 cup powdered sugar

1 8 oz. cream cheese

1 small container of whipped topping

Bottom layer:

28 crushed Oreos

1 stick melted butter

Fill Springform pan with the layers. Chill 2-3 hours before serving. Top with whipped topping.

For Graduations

1. At the end of summer, buy beach towels. They make great presents and you can have them monogrammed.
2. Buy coffee shop gift cards or gas cards, if the student will attend college far from home. Rolls of quarters are also a great idea if they plan to use a Laundromat.
3. Stock up on inspirational books at your local bookstore.
4. Know that it's OK to just send a card with your best wishes and a promise of prayer depending on your relationship with the graduate.

For New People on Your Church Staff

Try some of these ideas to help new staff wives make an easier transition to your church and community.

1. Provide a list of important numbers for local doctors and dentists as well as a reliable hairdresser.
2. Make a map of the area, highlighting major roads and landmarks like the church, grocery store, and schools.
3. Act as a tour guide for your city. Point out places of interest such as the post office, schools, and great shopping stops. Treat them to lunch at a favorite spot.

4. Make a box of recipes and provide a basket of the dry ingredients needed to fix each one.

5. Prepare food for their freezer.

6. Schedule a playdate with kids whose ages match their children's.

7. Provide a church directory with all staff pictures marked so they can get to know names and faces.

Impromptu Hospitality

Sometimes people stop by unannounced or your hubby calls and tells you he invited some people over to visit. By throwing together some fun snacks, you can feel better prepared and welcome your guests de-stressed and ready to enjoy a time of fellowship.

The following recipes require pantry staples and things you normally have in your fridge—perfect items to keep on hand for those unexpected drop-in guests.

Appetizers:

HOT WING DIP (It's way better than it sounds!)
2 cans cooked, chopped chicken
    (about 3-4 breasts)
1 package cream cheese
2 cups shredded cheddar or jack cheese
1 small jar of orange-colored hot wing sauce
    (any brand)
1 cup ranch dressing
Mix together and cook in a casserole dish at 350° until bubbly. (About 20 min.) Serve with baked corn chips.

STROMBOLI (May serve as a main dish.)
1 can refrigerated pizza dough
Pepperoni
Sliced ham
Salami
Mozzarella cheese
1 egg
Unroll dough and cover with a layer of each ingredient starting with the pepperoni and finishing with the shredded cheese. Start at the wide edge and roll up, pinching the dough together to seal. Place on a cookie sheet and brush with beaten egg. Cook at 350° for about 20 min. or until crust is brown.

ROTEL® CHEESE DIP
1 block of Velveeta®
1 can Rotel tomatoes
1 lb. sausage
Corn chips
Cook and drain sausage. Mix with melted Velveeta and Rotel. Cook in a crock pot to keep it melted.

BEAN DIP
1 can refried beans
shredded cheese
corn chip scoops
Spread beans in microwave safe dish and cover with cheese then microwave until cheese is melted. Excellent with corn chip scoops.

PIZZA DIP

8 oz. cream cheese

8 oz. pizza sauce

1 tbsp. onion

2 tbsp. green pepper

1 small can sliced black olives

1 cup mozzarella

Pepperoni

Mash cream cheese in bottom of pan. Spread pizza sauce over top. Grate 1 tablespoon of onion and 2 tablespoons of a green pepper for next layer. Add 1 small can of sliced black olives and 1 cup of mozzarella. Top with pepperoni. Bake at 350° for 20 minutes. Serve with corn chip scoops.

CHILI DIP

Canned chili or leftover homemade chili

Sour cream

Cheese

Spread chili in microwave safe dish. Cover with sour cream then shredded cheese. Microwave until cheese melts. Serve with corn chip scoops.

SAUSAGE CREAM CHEESE CRESCENT ROLLS

2 cans crescent rolls

1 package cream cheese

1 lb sausage

Cook sausage and drain. Mix in a block of cream cheese until melted. Unroll one can of crescents into a 9x13pan. Spread sausage cheese mixture across crescent rolls and top with the other can of crescents. Bake at 350° until brown. About 15 min.

SAUSAGE BALLS

10 oz. grated cheddar

2 and 1/2 cups Bisquick®

1 lb. sausage

Mix ingredients together by hand and shape into balls. Place on baking sheet and cook at 375° till slightly brown. Makes 2-3 dozen.

Main Dishes That Feed a Crowd:

DELI SANDWICHES

Offer a selection of meats, cheeses, and fixings with different types of bread. Let everyone fix his or her own. Provide chips, dip, and pickle spears.

CLAM CHOWDER

½ stick margarine

1 medium onion

1 can minced clams

3 cans cream of potato soup

2 cans New England clam chowder

1 quart half and half

Melt margarine and sauté the onion. Put in Crock-Pot and add clams, cream of potato soup, New England clam chowder, and half and half. Cook on low for four hours. Stir about every 30 minutes to prevent sticking.

Desserts

EASY COOKIES

Serve the ready-to-bake kind with ice cream.

DUMP CAKE

1 can crushed pineapple (Do not drain.)

1 can cherry pie filling

1 box yellow cake mix

1 cup chopped pecans

2 sticks margarine

Mix pineapple and cherry pie filling together and pour in a 10x13 pan. Sprinkle cake mix on top. Dot with 2 sticks of melted margarine. Sprinkle nuts on top. Bake at 350° for 1 hour.

COOKIES FROM BOX CAKE

1/4 cup brown sugar

¾ cup oil

1 egg

1 pkg. cake mix (any flavor, any brand)

1/2 cup chopped nuts, raisins, or
    chocolate candies

Mix ingredients. Drop on ungreased cookie sheet. Bake at 350° for 10 to 15 minutes.

CANDY BAR CAKE

1 box chocolate cake mix

1 jar of caramel ice cream topping

1 can of condensed milk

Whipped topping

Candy pieces

Bake a chocolate cake mix as directed. While warm poke holes in the cake and then mix together the caramel and condensed milk and pour over the cake. After cake has cooled, ice with the whipped topping and sprinkle with candy pieces or chocolate chips.

CRESCENT ROLL DESSERT/ DANISH

2 cans crescent rolls

2 8 oz. packs of cream cheese (soft)

1 cup confectioner's sugar

Icing:

1 cup confectioner's sugar

2 tsp. vanilla

2 tablespoons milk

Mix cream cheese and confectioner's sugar. Spray 9 by 13 casserole dish with cooking spray. Roll out one can of crescent rolls into bottom of dish. Spread mixture over rolls. Roll out other can of crescent rolls on top of mixture. Bake at 350° for about 25 minutes. Mix together icing ingredients and drizzle over hot crescent rolls.

Dear Minister's Wife:

Women today feel overwhelmed and burned out. You have additional demands and expectations unique to your role. Women in your church look to you for guidance and encouragement but you can't minister to all of them. That's why I'd like to tell you about *Journey*, a devotional magazine for busy women.

Journey's devotionals, articles, and special features provide inspiration and encouragement while equipping women to apply biblical principles in their everyday lives. Even the busiest women find that *Journey* provides an easy and inviting way to develop meaningful, consistent quiet times with God.

Through relevant, biblically-based messages that resonate with women today, *Journey* invites readers to draw close to Jesus, sit at His feet, and be transformed by His presence.
They will learn to depend on God for more and you for less. *Journey* is designed to be a tool churches can use to help disciple and equip women to serve in the church and impact their communities for Christ.

LifeWay understands that being a minister's wife is not easy, and we want to thank you for the important role you play. We on the Women's Ministry team at LifeWay recognize your service to your family, your church, and the body of Christ, and we greatly appreciate you. I hope that along with the other women in your church, *Journey* will be a source of refreshment and encouragement for you.

May God richly bless you on your journey with Him.

Pam Nixon
Editor, Journey

hot topics

The following section addresses common concerns ministry wives raise. While we don't consider ourselves the authority on any of the issues, we do want to share our perspective.

Q: How can I deal with the financial strain that sometimes comes with serving in the ministry?

> **A:** Creating a financial plan or budget with your husband and agreeing to stick to it can go a long way to relieving money-related tensions. You can also alleviate the stress of unexpected expenses like shower gifts and deacon gifts by following our practical suggestions in the section Helpful Hints on page 110-114. In any case, remember not to complain about your husband's salary to people in your church. If anything needs to be addressed concerning his salary, you need to let him be the man and deal with the situation himself. Above all, God will provide what you need and will give you the wisdom to manage your finances.

Q: Are most of your friends other ministers' wives, women in the church, or ladies outside the church?

> **A:** Many people advise ministry wives to make their connections to women outside the church and to limit their relationships with women in the church. We do caution you to use discretion in forming relationships with anyone. We both have friends in our church and outside the church, but we do protect ourselves and them from knowing too much about our personal lives. It's especially important to build strong relationships with the other wives on staff at church. Unity and cohesion among wives strengthens the team that our minister husbands lead.

Q: My husband just graduated seminary and is looking for a church to pastor. What's expected of a new minister's wife?

    A: The answer to this question largely depends on your church situation. Follow your husband's lead and determine to present yourself as friendly, modest, and kind. Get to know the people in your church and develop a love for them. As you do, you will find your place and your ministry style. Always be quick to listen and slow to offer opinions. Let people get to know you and love you before you jump in to make changes and avoid the possibility of sounding like a know-it-all.

Q: How can I encourage the ministry wives in my church to get along?

    A: First, understand that even the most agreeable people don't always see eye to eye. The best thing you can do for the ladies in your sphere of influence is to pray for them; sometimes difficult attitudes point to underlying spiritual or personal issues. Remember, never talk about anyone behind her back; that causes disharmony and disunity and can negatively affect the entire church. Always remain cordial, even if you must politely agree to disagree. Your attitude can set the bar, silently encouraging others to treat one another with love and respect.

Q: What should I do when someone talks bad about my husband in front of me?

    A: Much of your response should depend on the situation and the people involved. One option is to try to laugh it off with a light joke before politely excusing yourself. Try something like, "Whoa, he may not be perfect, but he's my husband" or "Careful, that's my man you're talking about." In any case, the key is controlling anger so that you don't say something to escalate the issue. Remember, your attitude impacts how people perceive your husband.

Q: How do you handle women in your church who dress immodestly?

> **A:** First, understand that people who come to check out the teachings of Christianity at your church will often and understandably reflect a style of dress popular in the world. Be sure you are setting a good example with your own clothing and style. You may even want to plan a seasonal fashion show to help teach how it's possible to be in style and modest at the same time. Help your church find ways to incorporate style and modest clothing teaching in the elementary-age areas. Also, be sure that the teens hear how to reclaim modesty. If a certain situation requires you to speak with an individual about appropriate dress, be certain to speak to her privately and with love.

Q: What should I do when I don't feel like going to church anymore?

> **A:** Begin by identifying the source of those feelings. If they are tied to the amount of time you spend at church, talk to your husband and evaluate whether you can take a break from some extra activities that don't require your presence. If, however, you find your feelings are tied to issues with church members, staff, or your spouse, Scripture tells us that spiritual growth requires meeting together for corporate worship. Remember that it's easier to act your way into a feeling than feel your way into an action. Keep praying and listen to what God has to say about your schedule and resolving those feelings.

Q: How do you balance home life and participation in all church activities? Sometimes I feel like the boring little wife holding down the fort at home while my husband goes on great adventures.

> **A:** A minister's wife with kids in tow can't do all of the camps, mission trips, and retreats that her husband does. As you choose which events you should join your husband on, be sensitive to the fact that many of a minister's trips are part of his job. Stay behind if your presence (particularly if you take

the kids) might become a distraction. Attend when you can, but don't feel obligated to pack up your toddlers or school-age children every time your spouse needs to go out of town. Remember, too, that a little time apart is actually good for husbands and wives.

Furthermore, understand that your work as a wife on the home front is far from boring. More importantly, what you do empowers the work of the ministry. Don't let the enemy discourage you; find ways to make those times when your husband's out of town fun. Paint a room, go see your folks, or just enjoy fixing chicken nuggets for dinner five nights in a row!

transitional tips

While some ministers continue to serve the same congregation for decades, far more make numerous moves over the course of their careers. We hope the following suggestions will help you navigate such transitions.

Knowing When to Share

When your husband is talking to another church, you may naturally want to share the news with friends within your current church. Keep the news confined to as small a number as possible until you'e sure you are leaving. Remember, some people take a pastor's move personally and may feel abandoned by your husband's willingness to consider a new position. In any case, timing is very important. Once your husband accepts the new position and gives his okay to let others know about it, enlist the prayer support of those closest as you and your spouse break the news to your extended church family.

After the Resignation Is Announced

Following a formal announcement of your move, remember that God ultimately controls the changes in your family's lives. Should you face opposition to your announcement or even feel the sting of being suddenly ignored by close acquaintances, remind yourself that you wouldn't leave without God's direction. Stress to those you'll leave behind that although God's will sometimes requires tough changes, following Him is always the right thing to do. Thank people for the impact they made on your life, and remind them that God has someone else in mind to continue the work at their church. Focus on the positives as you enlist friends to pray for your transition and the new challenges your family will face. Commit to staying connected, which is easier than ever with email, instant messaging and online communities.

Preparing for the Move

Planning ahead makes those first days in a new space feel less intimidating. Before you pack any boxes, brainstorm a list of things you can do to help make the transition a little easier. Here are a few ideas to get you started:

- Always put clean sheets in the dresser drawer of each bedroom set so you'll have fresh bedding on arrival.
- Pack an open box with hand towels, soap, and bath tissue so the bathrooms will be usable as soon as you move in.
- If movers are packing for you, supervise them closely so that you can write information like "open first" on the boxes.
- Pack daily necessities in your car instead of the moving van.
- Allow small children to pack special toys, blankets, and stuffed animals in a convenient box or bag so they'll have some things to open while you unpack. A few "friends" will also help the new place feel more like home.

Coping When Left Behind

Sometimes Mom and the kids must stay and sell the house or finish out the school year before following Dad to his new job. When the situation is unavoidable, it's tough to remind yourself of the positives. Try to use the extra days to spend time with old friends and remember that God has everything from the sale of your home to your family's welfare under His control. As you wait, pray for your new church and ask for wisdom in the transition time. Remember that "this too shall pass," and one day the frustrations will fade to memory. When you have a set day to move, let people know and plan a time for friends to drop by for good byes. Prepare cards with your new contact information to give out.

Settling In

Give yourself time to acclimate to your new home. Don't stress over getting everything unpacked perfectly and immediately. Take your time and set a pace that allows you to sort your belongings and clean out anything you no longer need. Should people stop in to say "hello" or lend a hand, try not to panic over the state of your home. Let people who stop by see you as a normal person with lots to do. Make sure they know you really appreciate their help.

As you adjust to life in your new church, allow God time to show you where He wants you to serve. Instead of continually comparing the new church to your last, focus on the new and give yourself a chance to learn about and love your latest church family. Although you need to take time to develop friendships, don't hesitate to "show yourself friendly" (NKJV). Let people know you are interested in them and looking forward to building relationships within the church family.

Dealing with Emotion

When transitions happen, ministry families often experience a roller coaster ride of emotions. On one hand they may cry with the church family they leave behind and in the same day they may rejoice with their new church family who is excited about their coming. In every case, it's important that you depend on the Lord's guidance and not your feelings during a transition time.

Remember, too, that you must set the tone for how your family deals with a move. Encourage your children to talk about their feelings and remain sensitive to your husband's need to share; most everyone will deal with some degree of insecurity during a big change. Be careful to validate the feelings expressed by your family, even if they differ from your own. Acknowledge that they will miss old friends, but point out ways to stay in touch while finding new ones. Keep your family focused on the good things about a move and not just the difficulties. Consider what you can do to ease the way. Point out fun things about the new area where you'll serve. And most importantly, don't forget to pray with your kids about all the details of their lives: friends, school, sports, and hobbies.

leader guide

Welcome to *In Our Shoes … Real-Life Issues for Ministers' Wives by Ministers' Wives*! This leader guide provides directions for leading an optional eight-session group study. We're so glad you've agreed to facilitate this experience. Know that our prayers go with you as you undertake this exciting and important endeavor.

Prior to each meeting, please complete the assignments pertaining to that session's content. (Your first meeting will cover the material presented in chapter 1.)You don't need to know all the answers, but you do need familiarity with the material. In each get-to together, you will guide participants to better understand and apply the concepts and principles they've studied. More ideas are provided for you than you'll have time to use, so choose the questions and activities that best meet your setting and the needs of your participants.

GENERAL TIPS:
- Prior to the first meeting, pray about whom God wants you to invite to this group study (see the list of suggestions on pages 6-7). Contact those who you think might show interest and secure a comfortable meeting place. Remember, a group can consist of as few as two people. Make sure that each participant has a copy of this workbook at least one week prior to your first meeting. If possible, plan to meet on a weekly basis. Each gathering should last between 60-75 minutes.

- Inform members that they should read and complete chapter one's content prior to the first group meeting. Consider sending each participant a personalized note, letting her know you look forward to spending time with her throughout the study.

- Pray, pray, pray before each meeting. Encourage participants to pray specifically for each other during and after each group time.

- If possible, find a place to meet that keeps participants in a circular formation. We've found this is the best configuration for open group discussion.

- Always begin your times together with a reminder that anything shared in class should remain in class. (You'll also want to ask participants to sign the group covenant on page 143 during the first meeting.) Remember, everyone may not feel comfortable sharing in a group setting, because they might feel their private information could be repeated or used against them in some way. Do everything you can to nurture feelings of respect and security within the group. Gossip is not allowed under any circumstance.

- Be willing to invest in each participant. Remain sensitive to their individual needs, strengths, and weaknesses. Continue to call for volunteers to share and pray without pressuring the more reluctant. You may find it helpful to share your own experiences in times when conversation lags.

- Be aware that some people may feel a need to unload their dirty laundry or turn your meeting times into gripe sessions. Be ready to step in and turn the conversation, if necessary. If one person continually disrupts class in this way, speak privately with and pray with her.

SESSION ONE
Before the Session
1. Read and complete chapter one's content.
2. Provide nametags, felt tip markers, pens, copy paper, and light snacks for the first gathering. (You may want to choose a helper to assist you in providing snacks for subsequent meetings.) If time allows, create nametags shaped as high heels, flip-flops, and sandals.

3. If you plan to have a large group, enlist the help of a volunteer to keep up with attendance and contact information.
4. Pray over your meeting room and the names of the ladies who'll attend. Ask God to bless your time together and to give you wisdom as you lead.
5. Start and finish on time!

During the Session
1. Have participants fill out nametags and help themselves to refreshments as they come in. Make sure to welcome them each by name when possible. If you don't already have access to it, be sure to solicit contact information at this time.
2. Introduce yourself, explain why this study is important to you, and ask the ladies to introduce themselves and their ministry roles to the group. (Example: My name is Joy and my husband has served as the senior pastor at Community First for thirty-five years.)
3. Establish the following confidentiality guidelines:
   - Everything shared in the room stays in the room. Nothing is repeated outside the group.
   - No one has to share.
   - Discretion should be used. Eliminate the names of specific people or churches whenever possible.
4. Ask the women to turn to page 143 of their books and have them read and sign the group covenant.

5. Lead this ice-breaker activity. Divide the group into teams of 3 or 4 and hand each group a pen and piece of paper. Instruct each team to compile a list of as many different brands of shoes as possible. Set a time limit such as 3 minutes and then call for teams to share their lists. Say, Many different kinds of shoes flood the market—some affordable and some costly. Either way, they all go on people's feet and provide an important service. Point out that our callings to ministry are similar to the important role shoes play. They may all look a little different and have been received in different ways, but they each serve a purpose. God placed each of our callings on our lives, and it is up to us what we will do with the opportunities He's given.

6. Ask everyone to come back together and pray aloud for God's guidance over today's session.

7. Ask participants to briefly respond to the following questions. Set a time limit of 2-3 minutes per person. It may help to share your story first.

   • How did you get started in ministry?

   • How would you describe your ministry journey to this point?

8. Use the following questions and suggestions to guide your discussion according to your set time limits. Remember, it's important to honor a promise to conclude at a certain time.

• Read aloud the definition of "calling" from page 11. Discuss any aspects of the definition that surprised you or gave you new insight.

• Ask for a volunteer to read aloud 2 Peter 1:10-11. Discuss the chapter questions related to it (see p. 11). Ask: Is it possible to have a thriving ministry if you have not solidified your calling? Why or why not?

• Discuss the four adjectives people generally use to describe their call to serve as ministry wives (see p. 13). Encourage participants to share which of the four parties they'd be most likely to attend based on their own experiences with the call to ministry.

• Refer to the blank invitation on page 16. Discuss the various ways participants serve in the work of the Kingdom. If possible, write specific tasks on a whiteboard or poster. Affirm them in their efforts.

• Ask: Using what you've learned from this chapter, how would you encourage the wife who resists her calling? Or, If you struggle to embrace the ministry as your own, what type of encouragement do you need to experience?

• Discuss some things all believers are called to do such as witness, tithe, pray and bear one anothers' burdens.

• Say, Some common advice for potential ministers, "If you can do anything else and be satisfied, then do it." Ask: Do you agree or disagree with this advice? Why?

- Close in prayer, thanking God for the calling He has placed on each life present. Ask Him to provide direction for any who struggle to own their callings. (Note: While you may choose to ask for a volunteer to pray, remember that just because all participants are married to ministers does not mean they are all comfortable praying aloud.)

10. Remind participants to read and complete chapter 2 before the next meeting time. If anyone still needs a copy of the book, help her secure one before the next group meeting.

After the Session

1. Personally thank each woman for her participation. You may do this through face-to-face conversations, phone calls, e-mails, or even the mail.

2. If possible, make yourself available for further, individualized discussions. Remember that many people participate in group Bible studies in part to make new friends. Watch the time so that everyone can share during this first session.

SESSION 2

Before the Session

1. Read and complete chapter two's content.

2. Pray over the session.

3. Provide nametags, whiteboard or tear sheets, markers, and light snacks.

During the Session

1. Have participants fill out nametags and help themselves to refreshments as they come in. Make sure to welcome them each by name.

2. Lead this ice-breaker activity: Ask for volunteers to respond to these questions: What type of shoe would you say best represents your life at the moment? Why? (Ex. I'm a running shoe because I am always running all over the place to keep up with my kids.)

3. Pray for God's guidance over this session and remind everyone of their confidentiality agreement.

4. Direct attention to the markers and white board or tear sheets set up at the front of the room. Ask for two volunteers to write on the board or sheets. Have the group brainstorm a list of all the roles they fill at church. The first volunteer should write these on the left side of the board or on the first tear sheet. On the right side, have the second volunteer list roles participants fill outside the church.

5. Use the following questions and suggestions to guide your discussion according to your set times.

- Say, We must glorify God in our discussions. As we discuss the frustrations that sometimes accompany our callings, we may find it tempting to "air our dirty laundry." Ask, Why is doing this ineffective? Agree to stay on track.

- Discuss the varied answers to the white-board exercise. Empathize with the group on the difficulty of juggling so many different things. Encourage one another in your shared commitments to family, church, work, and community.

- Discuss reasons why some women hide behind labels and relationships rather than defining themselves in terms of who they are. (see p. 22)

- Consider the nametag activity on page 22. Ask, If you could fill out this nametag with words and phrases designed to help people see you as you'd like to be known what would you say?

- Consider the paragraph listing biblical women who believed. (see p. 24). Ask, What different, modern ministries do you think each of these women may have chosen to actively support? (Ex. Rahab might support Celebrate Recovery. Mary might work with the Crisis Pregnancy Center.)

- Discuss the Action Step on page 25. Challenge participants to share ways they can intentionally apply Scripture's promises to their lives. Invite group members to give Scripture memorization tips.

- Ask each woman to share one thing from this chapter's content that she's found encouraging. Prompt her to explain why.

6. Close in prayer, asking each person to praise God specifically for who they are in Him. Ask them to complete this sentence "Thank You Lord…," acknowledging His wisdom in making each of them a unique, gifted individual.

7. Remind participants to complete chapter 3's content prior to the next meeting.

8. Start and finish on time.

After the Session

1. If possible, send each woman a note, text or e-mail telling her one thing that you appreciate her as an individual and reminding her of one thing God has to say about her.

Ex: Jeanne, I just wanted to thank you for always being our group encourager. I really admire that about you. God's Word says, "A merry heart doeth good like a medicine" (Prov. 17:22, KJV), and I'm grateful to you for being 'good medicine' for our group. I'm praying for you. Blessings! Betty."

SESSION 3
BEFORE THE SESSION

1. Read and complete chapter 3's content.
2. Pray over the session.
3. Provide light snacks, paper plates, and markers for each participant. You may also need a marker and tear sheet as well as a CD player and worship CD.

During the Session

1. Have participants help themselves to refreshments as they come in. Make sure to welcome them each by name.

2. Lead this ice-breaker activity: Distribute a paper plate to each participant, instructing them to draw a happy face on one side of the plate and an angry or sad face on the other. Read through a list of different scenarios and direct group members to hold up their plates reflecting the emotion they feel toward each one. Your list might include such things as church pot luck dinners, deacon meetings, free ball game tickets, financial planning meetings, family vacations, starting new women's Bible studies, helping out in the church nursery, and wearing choir robes. (Don't forget to hold up your own plate.)

3. Ask for a volunteer to pray aloud for God's guidance over this session.

4. Write the word blessing down the left hand side of a whiteboard or tear sheet. Ask participants to help you make it into an acrostic by suggesting words that bring to mind different blessings of ministry. (Example: B-baked items like bread that people bring to you)

5. Use the following questions and suggestions to guide your discussion.

• Ask participants to share the name of someone who has influenced their spiritual walk. (Refer to the activity on page 32).

• Discuss some of the funniest things about church traditions with which you grew up, taking care not to condemn or insult a particular church or denomination. Focus on how times and cultures change. Ask, What church traditions do we now observe that may one day become obsolete? What must we not allow to become obsolete in our churches?

• Ask group members to share similarities or differences they share with church leaders from their pasts. Say, We can learn from our predecessors. Likewise, younger women within your congregations will also look up to you.

• Discuss whether or not ministers' wives have the right to feel bitter. Encourage them to explain their reasoning.

• Ask for a volunteer to read aloud Psalm 103:1-2, which follows a passage in which the psalmist laments the tough times on which he's fallen. Ask, What can we learn from the psalmist's response to pain?

• Discuss the Fun Flip exercise on page 36. Ask, What do you do to brighten your attitude when feeling discouraged or angry?

• Say, Pretend I am a fellow ministry wife experiencing bitterness toward people who've hurt my husband or children. What advice would you offer me to help me choose blessing over bitterness?

• Go around the room and ask each participant to share her favorite thing about being married to a minister.

6. Encourage the ladies to continue through the study material and remind them of the next meeting time.

7. If possible, play a praise and worship song or hymn to close with a time of thanksgiving.

8. Remind participants to complete chapter 4's content prior to next session.

After the Session

1. Send a text or e-mail to group members, encouraging them to press through any difficulties that will arise as they work to complete their material for the next session.

SESSION 4

Before the Session

1. Read and complete chapter 4's content.

2. Pray over the session.

3. Provide coffee and refreshments, a white board or tear sheet and markers, and a pair of women's cross trainers (tennis shoes). You may also choose to bring a funny prize for the winner of the ice-breaker activity.

During the Session

1. Have participants help themselves to refreshments as they arrive.

2. Lead this Ice-breaker activity: Hold up tennis shoes and identify them as cross trainers. Divide participants into pairs and challenge them to complete the following sentence, "My life as a ministry wife is like a cross trainer because ..." Award a funny prize for the most creative answer.

3. Ask for a volunteer to pray aloud for God's guidance over this session.

4. Use the following questions and suggestions to guide your discussion.

• Address the issue of busyness in the life of a ministry wife. Ask participants to share their favorite ministry-related activities.

• Discuss the importance of spiritual health. Ask, What danger does busyness pose to spiritual health?

• Ask, What are the top three reasons that we should make our spiritual health a priority?

• Point out the Fun Flip on page 46. Encourage participants to brainstorm a list of suggestions for making quiet time with the Lord a priority. Share any resources and personal ideas that members have for making that time effective.

• Ask for a volunteer to read the quote on page 47. Discuss how good can become the enemy of best, sharing examples as possible.

• Share one thing that the self-evaluation questions on page 50-51 revealed about how you might need to change in order to strengthen your relationship with God. Ask participants to share their responses.

• Remind participants of the discussion on page 48-49 regarding how negativity and a poor perception of self can keep people from experiencing the fullness of the Holy Spirit. Ask, What can we do to make sure our lives are surrendered to the Holy Spirit's control? What are the greatest hindrances to full surrender?

- Ask, What things do women supposedly crave? (i.e., chocolate; shopping). Write answers on a whiteboard or tear sheet. Ask, What should we as believers crave? As women share their responses, use the marker to draw a large cross over the previous list. State that craving Jesus should take precedence over anything else.

5. Divide the group into pairs. Ask participants to share with their partners at least one of the questions from page 50-51 to which they answered in a way that conflicts with God's best for them. Encourage them to pray for each other about their weaknesses. Remind them that what's discussed in group time stays in group time.

6. Close by praying Psalm 63:1-2 over the group.

7. Remind participants to complete chapter 5's content prior to the next session.

After the Session

Make note of anyone who has missed a previous session and contact her with encouragement to persevere. Assure her she can pick up with session 5's material without worrying about any missed reading.

SESSION 5
Before the Session

1. Read and complete chapter 5's content.
2. Pray over the session.
3. Provide refreshments and a different color or type of shoelace for each participant (check your local arts and crafts store).

During the Session

1. Have participants help themselves to refreshments.
2. Lead this Ice-breaker activity. Pass different color or styles of shoelaces to each participant instructing the ladies to make one knot in their lace for every year of their marriage. Then ask participants to find someone in the room whose number of knots matches her own lace. Encourage them to find out where and when one another were married.
3. Ask for a volunteer to pray aloud for God's guidance over this session.
4. Remind group members not to use this session to bash their husbands. Encourage them to focus on strengthening their marriages through personal change.
5. Use the following questions and suggestions to guide your discussion.

- Ask participants to share their "characteristics of a healthy marriage."
- Ask, What factors bring pressure into your life that you feel others in ministry don't have to overcome?
- Ask for a show of hands as to who has ever had a problem with their husband's

ministry's encroaching on family life. We've all been there; don't hesitate to raise your own!

- Discuss areas where jealousy and bitterness can creep into lives in regard to our marriage relationships. Ask a volunteer to read Galatians 5:19-21, Proverbs 14:30, and Ephesians 4:31-32. Have participants offer suggestions of how they can apply these passages to the way they handle bitter or jealous feelings.

- Ask participants to share their favorite tips to a healthy marriage (see pp. 60-62). Say, Share a situation that highlights the wisdom of this tip.

- Point out his needs/ her needs lists on page 62. Ask, What surprised you about these lists?

- Lead group to share examples of how they each struggle not to think of Ephesians 5:22-33 in if/then terms. Be prepared to share first.

- Ask, What did you learn from the triangle illustrations on marriage? (see p. 66.)

- Read aloud Ephesians 1:18-20. Say, The same power that raised Jesus from the dead is the same power we can apply to our marriages. How does it feel to know that resurrection power is available to help with the day-to-day issues you as a ministry wife face?

6. Divide the group into the pairs they formed at the session's beginning. Ask them to pray together specifically over one another's marriage. Suggest that they keep one another's shoelace from the opening exercise, using it as a reminder to keep praying throughout the week.

7. Close in prayer.

8. Remind participants to complete chapter 6's content prior to the next session.

After the Session

Pray for each marriage represented in your group.

SESSION 6

Before the Session

1. Read and complete chapter 6's content.

2. Pray over the session.

3. Provide refreshments, blank note cards, and pens.

During the Session

1. Have participants help themselves to refreshments as they come in.

2. Lead this Ice-breaker activity: Hand a note card and pen to each participant. Say, Rank your family members in order of who consistently gets their shoes the dirtiest. Then ask for a couple of volunteers to share their lists. Point out that while raising kids is messy business, it also comes with triumphs. Go around the group, asking participants to respond to the question, What one thing do you most appreciate about each of your children?

3. Ask for a volunteer to pray over the session.

4. Remind everyone of the group covenant. Encourage them to refrain from using names if they need to share a particular frustration.

5. Use the following questions and suggestions to guide your discussion.

- Ask for a volunteer to explain the correlation between mom's and her kids' attitudes. Ask the group to explain, basing answers on their own experiences, why they agree or disagree with the statement "mom sets the tone of the home."

- Brainstorm a list of blessings that come with raising children in ministry.

- Turn to chapter 6 and starting on p. 68 read through the list of seven action steps you can take to meet the challenges of raising ministry kids. Share which of the steps most spoke to your experiences. Explain how you plan to start applying that step—even if your children are now grown.

- Ask for volunteers to share a time when someone particularly blessed or encouraged them by helping them with the kids. Encourage them to point out such blessings to their children as appropriate.

- Ask, What steps can you take to help make Sunday mornings easier? You may choose to begin by offering helpful hints of your own.

- Ask participants to each share a piece of funny or bad advice they've received in regards to child rearing. Ask, What should we do when someone gives us a piece of advice that reflects a traditional expectation instead of God's desires for our kids?

- Ask participants to share some practical ways they help their children deal with difficult peer situations. Encourage them to make one-on-one time for each of their children. Remind them that sometimes their kids just need a listening ear.

- Share a neat way that people have shown appreciation for your family. Go around the room, asking each participant to do the same.

Divide the group into pairs. Ask them to pray together specifically over one another's children. Encourage them to share specific concerns regarding each child.

Close in prayer.

Remind participants to complete chapter 7's content prior to the next session.

After the Session

Via e-mail or notes, challenge group participants to connect with each of their children this week to encourage them and share their love. Say, Before you hang up the phone, seal an envelope, or say goodbye, make sure to say, "I love you." Remind them that this counts for grown kids, too!

SESSION 7

Before the Session

Read and complete chapter 7's content.
Pray over the session.
Provide coffee and refreshments, a white board or tear sheet, and markers.

During the Session

1. Have participants help themselves to refreshments as they come in.

2. Lead this ice breaker activity: Ask participants to name Christian leaders from the news who drew the media's eye and cast a negative light on the ministry. (i.e., Mary Winkler; Jimmy Swaggart). Write responses on the white board or tear sheet. Point out that the fall of a religious leader makes big news, a fact lending support to the necessity of a discussion on spiritual warfare.

3. Ask for a volunteer to pray over this session's discussions.

4. Use the following questions and suggestions to guide your discussion.

   • Say, Spiritual warfare is sometimes more intense for people in ministry than for those outside it. Allow members to agree or disagree. Highlight the three main reasons why those in ministry often find themselves the targets of warfare (see pp. 83-84). Ask participants to share other possible reasons.

   • Encourage participants to suggest times and situations in which they feel particularly vulnerable to spiritual warfare.

   • Lead a discussion comparing and contrasting consequences and warfare. You may want to share some different scenarios and have people call out whether they think it is warfare or just consequences.

   • Ask, how can our poor choices impact the lives of those around us? Encourage discussion about how our positive choices can help lead people to Christ.

   • Refer to the statements on page 85 and ask, What might a life without any spiritual warfare suggest about a person's spiritual health? Allow participants to share whether they agree or disagree with the ideas presented in the paragraph.

   • Request a show of hands identifying participants whose husbands sometimes suffer with "holy hangovers." Ask, What can we do to help our husbands when they face spiritual warfare? How can we encourage and replenish them?

   • Ask for a volunteer to read Ephesians 6:10-18 aloud. Ask participants to share their favorite parts of the verses and to explain why.

5. Divide participants into pairs. Ask them to share with one another a label they assigned to a fiery arrow on page 91. Have the pairs pray over one another's specific situations.

6. Thank the participants for their faithfulness in attending and completing their assignments.

7. Remind women to complete chapter 8's content prior to the next session. Tell them that you'll have a special surprise to celebrate the conclusion of the study.

After the Session

Use the Ephesians 6:10-18 passage to create a small card or bookmark. Laminate them at a copy supply or office store and mail one to each participant. Encourage them to find strength from this Scripture.

SESSION 8
Before the Session

1. Read and complete chapter 8's content.
2. Pray over the session.
3. Provide special refreshments and a white board or tear sheet and markers. Provide appropriate supplies and/or professionals for your selected "Girlfriends" activity.*

During the Session

1. Have participants help themselves to refreshments as they come in. Make sure to start on time to accommodate your "Girlfriends" activity.
2. Lead this ice-breaker activity: On a white board or tear sheet at the front of the classroom, draw a stick figure of a woman. As participants arrive, encourage them to label the stick figure with characteristics that make a good friend.
3. Ask for a volunteer to pray over the session.

4. Use the following questions and suggestions to guide your discussion.

- Ask for volunteers to share any insights they received from looking at the positive and negative characteristics of friendship presented on page 97. Add positive qualities to the stick figure illustration on the board.

- Look on page 96 and discuss the advice participants have received on the subject of developing friendships within the church. Ask, what friendship related struggles do you face?

- Discuss the role past betrayals may play in building new friendships. Make sure to encourage participants to hand their pain over to the Lord asking Him to help them move past the hurt.

- Ask, How would you encourage another minister's wife who feels lonely and isolated?

- Ask participants to share their responses to "To whom are you accountable?" on page 107. Share a personal story of how a friend has held you accountable, encouraging others to do the same.

- Ask, How do you like to spend time hanging out with friends? Point out the value of time together as a friendship building time as a lead into the "Girlfriend" activity.

"GIRLFRIEND" ACTIVITY SUGGESTIONS:

- Decorate flip-flops with paint and ribbons and do-dads.
- Make key chains out of beads, hemp, decorations, and silver key rings.
- Create picture frames using craft-store starter frames, paint, buttons, or decoupage words from magazines or even old hymnals. (Take a group picture and send one to each member for her frame.)
- Enlist the help of some professionals in your church to help give one another pedicures and manicures.
- Enlist the help of some professionals in your church to help give facials or makeovers.

5. Close your "Girlfriend" activity by reminding participants to use their craft item or next manicure or facial to remind them that they are not alone but loved and supported by fellow ministry wives who walk in their shoes.

6. Place a chair in the center of the room and ask for a volunteer to sit in it. (If your group is larger than 15 you may want to divide into smaller sub groups for this closing prayer time.) Go around the room and have everyone say a statement of affirmation about the woman in the chair. Then have one lady pray for the person in the center. Take turns until everyone has sat in the center chair.

7. Thank the group for their faithfulness in attending and encourage them to stay in touch. Remind them of the Helpful Hints, Hot Topics, and Transitional Tips on pages 110-128. Encourage them to read through them as they continue to strive for abundant life in ministry.

Dear Pastor's Wife,

I'm certain you've met the perfect woman. You know, the one with all the answers. Her husband talks about how beautiful and wonderful she is, and her children say she's the most magnificent mom ever. The ultimate bargain shopper, she has a job outside the home that allows her to share with the needy. She sews clothes for everyone in the house, and her soft, kind words are laced with music. She's giddy with joy over her wonderful life! You know the one I mean. The one God pictured in His book of wisdom, the notorious Proverbs 31 woman.

As a woman in full-time ministry over 20 years, sometimes I've felt I'm expected to be like her. My guess is that you can fully relate. I've learned my original interpretation of that Scripture was way off by getting to know other women of the Word as well as women of the world. I do'nt walk in the shoes of a minister's wife; however, I do serve God in full-time ministry. God has called me to serve women devastated by abortion. Statistics tell us as many as 43 percent of the women in your church have had an abortion. Maybe you are one of them.

Recently, three pastors' wives confessed past abortions to me. Through tears they revealed secrets and the horror of letting their husbands down or disappointing women of the church who look up to them as an example. The truth is that the Enemy sells his lies to women, especially women leading women—the lie that we can't be real with one another, that we are to be perfect and are held to a higher standard than other women, that God can't use who we really are.

The truth is that women need women. Real women. God's Word is full of examples such as Mary's run to Elizabeth with her unexpected pregnancy and Ruth's commitment to Naomi at the loneliest time of her life.

My blessing to you, sister, is for the strength to be real and transparent, to trust God with who you are and His wise choice for your position in the body of Christ. My prayer is that your transparencies will open doors and that other women will follow you to freedom!

When I think of the wives of pastors, women who are engaged in full-time ministry not by always by choice but by marriage, Proverbs 31:29 comes to my mind: "Many women do noble things but you surpass them all." Thank you, surrendered sister, for your obedience and sacrifice.

Pat Layton, Author
Surrendering the Secret

group covenant

I, _____ , commit to following

the guidelines established for my group. I will strive to

glorify God by participating in group discussions and by

attending regularly. I will not repeat or discuss anything

shared within our group; instead, I will seek to encour-

age and pray for my sisters in ministry.

_____   _____

Signature   Date